WINNERS IN CHRIST

*Developing God's
Image of You*

NORMAN ROBERTSON

Winners In Christ
ISBN 0-9636898-4-3
Copyright © 1995 by
Norman Robertson
P.O. Box 3330
Matthews, North Carolina 28106

Published by NRM Publications
P.O. Box 3330
Matthews, North Carolina 28106

WINNERS IN CHRIST

by

Norman Robertson

NRM Publications
P.O. Box 3330
Matthews, North Carolina 28106
(704) 847-5999

ABOUT THE AUTHOR

Dr. Norman Robertson was born and educated in Britain, and in 1974 he moved to South Africa on contract as a professional engineer. Soon after arriving in the city of Durban, he was born again and baptized in the Holy Spirit at a full gospel service. As a result of his personal encounter with the Lord Jesus Christ, he answered the call of God upon his life to study and minister God's Word.

Norman studied and holds credentials with Moody Bible Institute, the Church of God, Rhema Ministries and the Elim Pentecostal Church of Great Britain. He is ordained with Covenant Ministries International and earned a Doctorate of Theology from the School of Bible Theology in San Jacinto, California.

For twelve years Norman was involved in full-time ministry in South Africa and was associate Pastor of a church that experienced supernatural growth to more than 15,000 members. At the Lord's direction he moved to the U.S. in 1992 to be a part of the great revival God is sending to America.

Norman lives in Charlotte, North Carolina, with his wife, Eleanor, and their two children, Jayne and Brian. As a dynamic Bible Teacher, Evangelist and author his anointed ministry stirs and strengthens local churches across the U.S. and Europe. His bold New Testament-style ministry imparts revelation knowledge truth that changes lives and equips the saints. Wherever he ministers the anointing of the Holy Spirit is present manifesting signs, wonders, healings and miracles just like in Bible days.

OTHER BOOKS BY NORMAN ROBERTSON

- *The Supernatural Church*
- *Improving Your Love Life*
- *Winners In Christ*
- *Ministering in the Power of the Holy Spirit*
- *Tithing*

To contact the author, write:

Norman Robertson
P.O. Box 3330
Matthews, NC 28106 U.S.A.

It is important to us that we continue ministering to you and helping you to grow spiritually, therefore we are sure you will want to order more anointed teaching materials.

For a complete list of our ministry products – **audio cassette tapes, books and videos** – write today, or call our ministry office at (704) 847-5999. God bless you!

Contents

True success in life is . . .

Becoming what God wants you to be
Doing what God wants you to do
Possessing what God wants you to have

Chapter One
Mirror, Mirror On The Wall

I have strength for all things in Christ Who empowers me
— I am ready for anything and equal to anything through
Him who infuses inner strength into me, [that is, I am self-
sufficient in Christ's sufficiency.]

Philippians 4:13 (AMP)

FEELINGS OF INFERIORITY and worthlessness are
widespread in today's world. Many people possess little or
no sense of personal worth. Countless individuals are plagued
with poor self-esteem, which is one of the most fundamental
problems affecting mankind.

This destructive condition is so common, it even affects
Christians. Many Christians quietly struggle under the oppres-
sive burden of a poor self-image. They are weighted down with
deep feelings of inadequacy and uselessness. However, this is
not a condition which Christians should be troubled with,
because we can live the overcoming life through Christ, and in
Him we can overcome all inferiority complexes.

Many years ago, a famous plastic surgeon, Dr. Maxwell
Malt, wrote a best-selling book, "New Faces—New Futures." It
was a collection of case histories of people for whom facial
surgery had opened the door to a new life. The author's theme
was that amazing personality changes can take place when a
person's face is changed.

However, as the years went by, Dr. Malt began to learn something else — not from his successes, but from his failures. He began to see patient after patient who, even after facial plastic surgery, did not change. People who were made not simply acceptable, but actually beautiful, kept on thinking and acting the part of the "ugly duckling." *They acquired new faces, but went on wearing the same old personalities.*

Worse than that, when they looked in a mirror, in spite of the fact that their friends and their family members could hardly recognize them, they would angrily exclaim to the doctor, "I look the same as before. You didn't change a thing." Although before-and-after photographs showed drastic differences, Dr. Malt's patients kept insisting: "My nose is the same." "My cheekbones are the same." "You didn't help at all."

In 1960, Dr. Malt wrote his best-seller, *Psycho-Cybernetics.* He was still trying to change people, not by correcting jutting jawbones or smoothing out scars, but by helping them change the pictures they had of themselves in their minds.

In his book, Dr. Malt commented that it seems as if every *personality* has a face. This *emotional face* of personality seems to be the real key to change. If it remains scarred and distorted, ugly and inferior, then the person continues to act out a role, regardless of the change in his physical appearance. But if the face of his personality can be reconstructed, if the old emotional scars can be removed, the person can be changed.

All of us could confirm this by our experiences with people, as well as our knowledge of ourselves. It is absolutely amazing the way self-image influences our actions, attitudes, and relationships with other people.

Where there is no vision, the people perish.

Proverbs 29:18 (KJV)

The true vision of you and your life comes from God, but Satan will do all he can to provide a counterfeit. With the wrong kind of vision about yourself, a picture of yourself as inferior and unable, you will surely self-destruct, and God's great plan for your life will not be fulfilled.

A strong and healthy self-image which is in accord with God's Word will lead to personal freedom.

Many people are imprisoned by a poor self-image. They will never attempt much, because they don't see themselves as able to accomplish anything. Freedom means not being in bondage, which comes in many forms.

I know people who need to be set free from despair in order to experience joy, from problems to know tranquillity, from loneliness to fullness of life, from rejection to acceptance, from inferiority to a positive self-image. Others need to be freed from the past to be able to enjoy the present. They are so accustomed to failure that they expect it.

*The Good News of the Gospel is that **God created you to be a success!***

God does not make failures!

It is not His nature to make failures, because God never fails!

You can become that beautiful person God created you to be. You are to be used of God to do wonderful things. Jesus said, "You are the salt of the earth...the light of the world" (Matthew 5:13,14). Life for you is not over, you are not washed up, you are not too old. You have not made too many mistakes!

David committed the sins of adultery, murder, and cover-up. When he repented and came clean with God, he discovered that God had never stopped loving him and wanted to continue to use him. God will use you, also. *Believe it!*

There is no greater thing than to be used of God!

There is no greater thing than to be used of God!
True success in life is...
Becoming what God wants you to be
Doing what God wants you to do
Possessing what God wants you to have

World's Best Sermon

There was a minister named Russell Conwell, who years ago preached what many consider the world's greatest sermon. It has been preached more times than any other message. It has been duplicated on tapes, written in books, and read by people all over the world. It was so good, even those who didn't believe in God discovered and used it for the wisdom it contained. The title is "Acres of Diamonds," and the message is this:

A man had a farm, but it wasn't enough. He wanted to be rich. He wanted to find great wealth. So he sold his farm to travel around the world in his quest for the great treasure he desired.

In the meantime, the man who bought the farm was out by the river one day. He happened to look down just as the sun caught something sparkling on the ground. He picked it up and discovered it was a beautiful diamond.

That one diamond turned out to be one of the most valuable diamonds ever discovered, and the farm became the world's most famous diamond mine.

The original owner was traveling all over the world to find his riches, but they were in his own backyard all the time — he just didn't know it.

People travel all over the world to find their place and purpose in life and to capture success. But all along it is right inside of them, like a treasure waiting to be discovered and used for great things!

As you look into the mirror in the morning, what do you really see looking back at you — a winner or a loser, a success or a failure, a victor or a victim?

Whatever picture you have of yourself today, *by applying the Bible-based principles in this book,* your life can be transformed from mediocrity to excellence, into the person of success and top performance God created you to be.

Chapter One Review

1. Countless individuals are plagued with poor self-esteem, which is one of the most fundamental problems affecting mankind.

2. It is amazing the way self-image influences our actions, attitudes, and our relationships with other people.

3. A strong and healthy self-image which is in accord with God's Word will lead to personal freedom.

4. You can become that beautiful person God created you to be.

You cannot consistently perform

in a manner which is inconsistent

with the way you see yourself.

Chapter Two
What Is Self-Image?

For as he thinks in his heart, so is he.

Proverbs 23:7

SELF-IMAGE REFERS to our personal evaluation or opinion of our worth, competence, and importance. It includes our thoughts, feelings, and attitudes toward ourselves.

Your self-image is the concept or picture you have of yourself. It is the way you think of yourself. It includes all the factors that have gone into your makeup — your inheritance and birth, infancy, childhood, teen years — and your experience of life right up to the present time. Self-image encompasses how you have been treated, how you have been trained, and how you have related to people all the years of your life.

Your self-image is based on a system of pictures and feelings you have put together about yourself.

The way you look at yourself and feel about yourself, deep in the heart of your personality, determines what you will be and what you will become. How you see and feel about yourself affects your relationships with other people, as well as your relationship with God.

Your parents, your environment, other people, and the events of your life all strongly influence the way you see yourself. Ultimately, however, no combination of events and circumstances can determine the image you hold of yourself. What shapes your self-image is not so much what happens *to* you, as what happens *in* you.

A wise man once said, "What lies behind us and what lies before us are tiny matters compared to what lies within us."

Self-esteem can be negative or positive. However, the vast majority of people possess a poor self-image. Many perceive themselves to be ugly when they are beautiful, unlovable when they are loved, unsuccessful when they have succeeded, useless when they are talented, worthless when they possess great value.

Self-esteem is a healthy condition which produces inward peace, godly contentment, and self-worth.

Lack of self-esteem is an unhealthy condition which hinders godly contentment, producing an underlying sense of frustration, inferiority, and inadequacy.

From Dunce To Genius

When Victor Seribriakoff was fifteen, his teacher told him he would never finish school and that he should drop out and learn a trade. Victor took the advice, and for the next seventeen years he was an itinerant worker, doing a variety of odd jobs. He had been told he was a dunce, and for seventeen years he acted like one.

When he was thirty-two years old, an amazing transformation took place in Victor's life. An evaluation revealed that he was a genius, with an I.Q. of 161. Guess what? He started acting like a genius! Since that time he has written books, secured a number of patents, and has become a successful, wealthy businessman.

The story of Victor Seribriakoff makes you wonder how many geniuses we have wandering aimlessly, acting like dunces, because someone told them they weren't too bright! Obviously, Victor did not suddenly acquire a tremendous amount of knowledge. What he did suddenly acquire was self-confidence. Consequently, he became more effective and productive.

Victor started expecting — and getting — different results in his life. *When he saw himself differently, he began acting differently.* "As a man thinketh, so is he."

You cannot consistently perform in a manner which is opposed to the way you see yourself.

Through God's Word, you can develop a new picture of yourself and begin moving into the realm of success. Stop looking at the ugly, distorted, defeated picture of yourself which Satan would have you see. Instead, see yourself the way God sees you — full of potential and promise. See yourself in the image of God. What is God like? Exactly like His Son, Jesus, who *was* and *is* the supreme Winner.

The picture you develop of yourself is crucial to your success or failure. God wants you to see yourself as His highest creation. He desires to pour His sensitivity and His wisdom into your life.

When you see yourself with the mind of Christ, you see a portrait of success — a picture that has been lovingly retouched by the Spirit of God to take out the blemishes of failure and the wrinkles of weakness, as He conforms you to the image of Christ. You see the perfect likeness of a winner, which is the way God sees you. He has a marvelous and thrilling photograph album of you. He sees all your high points, good qualities, and positive attributes.

Satan will try to show you a photograph of yourself at your worst. He tries to remind you what you were like at your weakest point. He takes a photograph of you when you are down and out, and that's what he holds in front of your face all the time. He even puts a magnifying glass in front of the defects and says, "Look how bad you look, how ugly you are!" His whole purpose is to give you a different image of yourself than how God sees you through Jesus Christ.

You are what you are and where you are because of what has gone into your mind. You change what you are and where you are by changing what goes into your mind.

Many people spend all their time concentrating on failure photographs of themselves, trying to cover up what is really a distorted picture. Through faith in God's Word, begin to see yourself through His eyes. Stop looking at the devil's picture of defeat, and focus on God's portrait of victory, prosperity, and success.

Here are some key questions you can ask yourself about your self-image, a personal evaluation checklist:

- Do you accept yourself just as you are?

- Would you say you love yourself? (Remember that Christ teaches us self love in Mark 12:31.)

- How do you handle correction and criticism? Do you take it personally or do you seek to learn from it?

- How comfortable are you when other people praise or compliment you?

- Do you talk to yourself and about yourself with respect or ridicule?

- Do you replay or rehash past failures?

- Do you replay or reinforce past victories and successes?

- Do you see yourself as a winner or a loser in life?

- Are you willing to begin to see yourself through the eyes of God and let God's Word shape your self-esteem?

Chapter Two Review

1. Your self-image is the concept or picture you have of yourself. It is the way you think of yourself.

2. What shapes your self-image is not so much what happens *to* you, but what happens *in* you.

3. A correct self-image is a healthy condition which produces inward peace, godly contentment, and self-worth.

4. Through God's Word, you can develop a new picture of yourself and begin moving into the realm of success.

5. By faith in God's Word, begin to see yourself through God's eyes. Stop looking at the devil's picture of defeat and concentrate on God's portrait of victory, prosperity, and success.

*One of Satan's greatest psychological
devices against the child of God
is inferiority, inadequacy and
a poor self-image.*

Chapter Three
Effects Of A Poor Self-Image

The thief does not come except to steal, and to kill, and to destroy. I have come that they may have life, and that they may have it more abundantly.

John 10:10

MANY PEOPLE HAVE POOR SELF-IMAGES because their ability, appearance, and intelligence have been ridiculed or questioned repeatedly by parents, teachers, friends, and others in authority. In this manner, Satan encourages them to see themselves through the negative eyes of others.

If their friends, family, and associates find fault with them, they get a distorted picture of who they really are. Then the devil has succeeded in robbing them of fulfillment in life.

Seven Causes Of A Poor Self-Image

1. Negative Experiences

As we have stated before, our present self-image is often the result of past conditioning. If we grew up with a lot of criticism, rejection, and disapproval, we may have picked up a negative self-image.

This kind of negative environment creates a tremendous sense of insecurity, inadequacy, and inferiority. A continual lack of emotional support or encouragement results in an attitude of self-contempt and rejection. When parents withhold love, acceptance, and forgiveness, a child grows up with a sense of poor self-esteem.

When people, in any relationship, are subjected to a spirit of condemnation, belittling, and disapproval, a gradual feeling of self-hatred and dislike can begin to develop in our opinion and evaluation of ourselves.

2. Negative Thinking

A poor self-image is often the consequence of prolonged negative thinking. Negative thinking is so deeply rooted in the thoughts of some people, it corrupts every area of their lives.

Our thinking patterns have an overwhelming impact upon our emotions, attitudes, and will. Many who suffer from poor self-esteem have an overly pessimistic view of themselves. They constantly reinforce their feelings of worthlessness and inferiority by ministering self-doubt and self-criticism.

Those who have a poor self-image only see themselves as deficient, useless, and inadequate, and this mental rut is extremely destructive. It only encourages the feelings of failure, despondence, and poor self-esteem.

3. Guilt

Poor self-esteem can often be the consequence of long-standing guilt. Unresolved guilt from the past can torture us with an overwhelming sense of failure, inadequacy, and wretchedness.

Many Christians cannot forget the sins of their past. They are haunted with memories of yesterday's mistakes. They have not fully accepted Christ's cleansing power and forgiveness, so they find it hard to forgive themselves or forget their former transgressions.

The nagging feeling of guilt creates self-condemnation, remorse, and a deep-seated disappointment in ourselves, which reinforces our sense of inferiority and failure.

4. Faulty Theology

One of the underlying causes of poor self-esteem among Christians is a distorted theological perspective. Some believers and preachers focus upon the scriptural revelation of man's sinful, fallen state, stressing the utter worthlessness of man. They mistakenly assume our previous sinful condition has forever rendered us insignificant and valueless before a holy, sovereign God.

They also attack any attitude of self-love or self-esteem as being a form of pride. As a result, they often embrace a false humility, which is nothing more than a demonically inspired, self-inflicted condemnation.

This distorted theology overlooks the believer's standing in Christ and emphasizes feelings of inferiority and inadequacy Instead of living in the confident reality of the righteousness of God in Christ, believers fearfully wallow in sin-consciousness.

5. Satan's Lies

Satan is a constant source of mental and emotional agitation. In Revelation 12:10, he is referred to as "the accuser of the brethren." He strives to destroy our godly self-esteem through accusation, criticism, and discouragement — all based on lies.

One of his greatest lies is that we are useless, inadequate, and of little value to God. He will even twist scriptures in his clever attempts to sow this falsehood. He works to promote this deception in order to undermine our godly self-esteem and cause us to withdraw from life and drown in despair.

Satan attempts to instill in us a sense of worthlessness and inferiority in order to quench our enthusiasm, hinder the work of God in our lives, and suppress our participation in the kingdom.

6. Life's Disappointments

Everyone grows up with idealistic expectations for their future. We all have our goals and dreams we would like to see fulfilled. However, many people fail to realize their great expectations. They find that life has dealt them a cruel hand.

Life is filled with setbacks, disappointments, and delays. Many people find the saying, "The best laid plans of mice and men often go astray" to be an appropriate characterization of their lives.

When we fail to achieve our goals, measure up to our expectations, or fulfil our dreams, we can gradually fall into a "failure syndrome." This undermines our self-confidence and reinforces a growing sense of inadequacy, incompetence, and inferiority.

7. Social Pressures

Social influences can have a tremendous impact upon our self-esteem. Social pressures can work to diminish or even destroy a healthy self-image.

Society imposes certain values and standards which can cause us to feel second-rate, inferior, and even abnormal. The cruel injustices, prejudices, and "value systems" of society can inflict deep wounds upon our sense of personal worth.

We can be rejected and held in contempt because of our race, ethnic background, social standing, lack of schooling, or religious upbringing. Many people grow up in a society which slowly robs them of their human dignity and worth. The tragic result is often a sense of poor self-esteem.

Symptoms Of A Poor Self-Image

A poor self-image is a cancerous condition which corrupts our emotions and actions, attitudes, thoughts, and values. It is the root of many destructive symptoms.

A poor self-image

- produces a deep sense of self-criticism, self-hatred, and self-rejection,

- creates a nagging feeling of being unwanted, unneeded, and unloved,

- causes gradual withdrawal and isolation from people,

- stifles initiative, quenches motivation, and reinforces the feelings of inadequacy, hopelessness, and weakness,

- is sometimes camouflaged by a negative, complaining, and argumentative spirit,

- causes jealousy, unforgiveness, resentment, intolerance, and suspicion toward others, and

- causes over-sensitivity, moodiness, depression, and introversion.

A poor self-image paralyzes your potential.

One of Satan's greatest psychological devices against the child of God is inferiority, inadequacy, and a poor self-image. This feeling shackles many Christians, in spite of wonderful spiritual experiences and their faith in God.

In a tape entitled, "Satan's Psychological Warfare," Christian psychologist Dr. James Dobson tells about a poll he took among a large group of women. Most of them were married, in excellent health, and happy. According to their own statements, they had happy children and financial security.

On the test, Dr. Dobson listed ten sources of depression. He asked the women to number them in the order of how the ten affected their lives. This is the list he gave them:

- absence of romantic love in your marriage
- in-law conflicts
- *low self-esteem*
- problems with children
- financial difficulties
- loneliness, isolation, boredom
- sexual problems in marriage
- health problems
- fatigue and time pressure
- aging

The women rated these by the amount of depression each produced. What came out way ahead of all the others? *Low self-esteem.* Fifty percent of these Christian women rated it first; eighty percent of them rated it in the top two or three.

Can you see the wasted potential of all these women? They are battling depression, which comes chiefly from the downward pull of feelings of low self-esteem.

A poor self-image spoils your relationships with other people.

Satan uses our nagging sense of inferiority and inadequacy to isolate us. He knows the most common way people cope with feelings of inferiority is to pull within themselves, to have as little contact with other people as they can, occasionally peeking out as the rest of the world goes by.

According to Jesus' own words in Mark 12:30,31, you are only able to give to others and love others when you first have surrendered your life to God, and then have a healthy (godly and biblical) opinion of yourself. Without a relationship with the Father, you devaluate yourself.

You become overly absorbed in and with yourself, because you are your own god, succeeding or failing by your own strengths or weaknesses. After tenaciously holding onto your sense of personal worth by your own abilities, you don't have anything left over to give to others.

Deep inside, the knowledge that you are living a self-absorbed life brings self-contempt and inferiority. Instinctively, you know you were created to love and to give, not to take and acquire.

Christians fall into this trap when they put other things before their relationship with God, neglecting study of His Word. It is the Word which affirms their significance and purpose in life.

Who are the hardest people to get along with? Those who don't like themselves. Because they don't like themselves, they don't like others, and they are hard to get along with. Therefore, they have few friends, if any, and their family life is miserable.

A poor self-image makes you ineffective for ministry.

What's the greatest obstacle that prevents members of the Body of Christ from functioning? What's the first thing people say when you ask them to do something in the church? Here are some common excuses:

"Teach a Sunday school class? I can't stand up in front of people."

"Share at the women's meeting, or at the men's meeting? Oh, I couldn't do that."

"Go knocking on doors in the Personal Evangelism Program. That would scare me to death."

"Me move in the gifts of the Spirit? Never!"

"Sing in the church choir? Why don't you ask Anne? She has a much better voice."

"I could never lay hands on the sick and pray for people."

Nothing undermines Christian service more than thinking so little of yourself that you never really give God a chance to use you. A poor self-image can keep you marching around in vicious circles of fear and uselessness.

Chapter Three Review

1. One of Satan's greatest psychological devices against a child of God is inferiority, inadequacy, and a poor self-image.

2. Seven contributors to a poor self-image are negative experiences, negative thinking, guilt, faulty theology, Satan's lies, life's disappointments, and social pressure.

3. A poor self-image produces a sense of self-criticism, self-hatred and self-rejection.

4. A poor self-image paralyzes your potential.

5. A poor self-image spoils your relationships with other people.

6. A poor self-image makes you ineffective for ministry.

Whether you realize it or not,

you have the power to choose

to make your life a failure or a success.

Chapter Four
The Me I See Is The Me I'll Be

There we saw the giants . . . and we were like grasshoppers
in our own sight, and so we were in their sight.

Numbers 13:33

WHY IS SELF-IMAGE SO IMPORTANT? Why is the
mental picture you hold of yourself so crucial a factor in
determining how far you will go in life and how happy you will
be along the way? Because your self-image shapes your choice
of a mate, your choice of friends, and your choice of leisure
activities. Your mental portrait determines your attitudes
toward yourself and the people around you, your capacity to
grow and learn, your actions in and reactions to life, and your
happiness or lack of happiness.

Nothing Can Stop You Except You

Background, education, circumstances — none of these
can hold you back unless *you* let them. Think, for example, of
Abraham Lincoln, who was elected President of the United
States in 1860.

He grew up on an isolated farm and had only one year of
formal education. In those early years, he was exposed to barely
half-a-dozen books. In 1832, he lost his job and was defeated in

the race for the Illinois legislature. The following year, he failed in business.

In 1834, Lincoln was elected to the state legislature; in 1835, his sweetheart died; and in 1836, he had a nervous breakdown. In 1838, he was defeated for Speaker of the House; and in 1843, he was defeated in a Congressional race. In 1846, he was elected to Congress; but in 1848, he lost the renomination.

In 1849, he was rejected for a federal land office appointment; and in 1854, he was defeated in a Senate race. In 1856, he was defeated for the nomination of Vice President; and in 1858, he was again defeated when he ran for the Senate.

The choices and decisions you make today will determine what you will have, be, and do in the tomorrows of your life!

Many people, both in the U.S. and abroad, consider Lincoln to be the greatest President of all time. Yet, it should be remembered how many failures and defeats marked his life, and how humble and unpromising his early beginnings were. It is obvious Lincoln made the choice to see himself according to God's plan, not his own successes or failures.

The more we allow our thinking to be transformed in accordance with the principles of the kingdom of God, the higher degree of success for Him we will achieve.

The story is told of an eagle which was kept as a pet for ten years, confined to the limitations of life in a cage. One day, his owner decided to set him free. The sky was his true realm. There would be no limits there, living where he was really created to live.

When the eagle was placed outside of his cage, it was a cloudy day, and he just stood there. Would he fly? Would he be able to fly? He hadn't flown for ten years. He wasn't familiar with the world outside of his cage.

As the eagle stood there looking around, the clouds parted, and the sun came out. A ray of sunlight encompassed the area where he was standing. When the eagle saw the light, it was as if it sparked new life in him. He opened up his wings, flapped them in place for a moment, and suddenly was airborne.

He was free! He had somehow received the power to operate in a new world, a world he had never known before. He had dared to begin a new life!

But those who wait on the Lord Shall renew their strength; They shall mount up with wings like eagles, They shall run and not be weary, They shall walk and not faint.

Isaiah 40:31

Some of you who are reading this have also been living a limited life — a life without meaning and power. Some of you don't know there is a whole new world for you to experience through the revelation knowledge of God's Word.

It's time for the "light" to hit you, too. It's time for you to stretch your wings and fly! It's time to be everything you were created to be, in and through the Lord Jesus Christ.

Ephesians, chapter 1, tells us of the love, respect, and honor in which God views us as His children:

- He has *blessed* us (v. 3).
- He has *chosen* us (v. 4)
- He has *predestinated* us (v. 5)
- He has *accepted* us (v. 6).
- He has *redeemed* us (v. 7).
- He has *forgiven* us (v. 7).
- He has a*bounded* toward us in wisdom (v. 8).
- He has *made known* to us the mystery of His will (v. 9).

- He has *sealed* us (v. 13).
- He has *enlightened* our understanding (v. 18).

Ephesians 2:6 tells us He has *raised* us to sit in heavenly places! To you, God says, "My child, I love you, I accept you, I care about you, I forgive you, I'm going to use you, and I am with you all the way." *So accept God's love and love yourself!*

Two Important Questions

Ask yourself two vital questions. First, "Do I really like myself?" And second, "Do I see myself as a capable person and what I am doing as worthwhile?"

The phrase, "Love your neighbor as you love yourself," is stated six times in the Bible (Leviticus 19:18; Matthew 19:19; Mark 12:31; Luke 10:27; Romans 13:9; and James 2:8). It is listed by Jesus as the second greatest commandment.

Even medical research has shown that we tend to act in harmony with our mental self-portrait. If we don't like the kind of person we are, we think no one else likes us either, and that influences our social life, our job performance, and our relationships with others.

Self-image has been defined as what we think, see, and feel ourselves to be. The concept of self-image was around long before the twentieth century. Approximately 3,000 years ago Solomon wrote:

For as he thinks in his heart, so is he.

Proverbs 23:7

You will never rise, you will never perform, you will never achieve, and you will never attain beyond your level of self-worth. What you think of yourself, your self-image or sense of self-worth, influences every part of your life.

Look around you at the people whom you admire for their lives of success and excellence. What do you see? More than likely you will see many of the following positive qualities.

- Personal relationship with Christ
- Right spiritual foundation
- Faith in God and His Word
- Walking in godly wisdom
- Drive, a high degree of motivation
- Courage, tenacity, and persistence
- Goals, a sense of direction
- Knowledge, and a thirst for it
- Good health
- Honesty and integrity in every aspect of life
- Optimism
- Sound judgment
- Enthusiasm
- Chance taking, the willingness to risk failure
- Dynamism, energy, and vitality
- Enterprise, willing to tackle tough jobs
- Persuasion, ability to sell
- Outgoingness, friendly
- Communication, articulate
- Receptive, alert
- Patient yet impatient; patient with others, yet impatient with the status quo
- Adaptability, capable of change
- Perfectionism, seeking to achieve excellence

- Humor, ability to laugh at life
- Versatility, broad interests and skills
- Individualism, strong self-esteem
- Love and respect for other people
- Creativity and imagination
- Perseverance and persistence
- Adventurous, with multiple interests
- Ability to recognize and break bad habits
- Independent thinker
- Full of compassion, with a desire to help hurting humanity
- Ability to hear God and the courage to obey

How many of these positive qualities do you see in your personality? Your mental picture of yourself is the key to your healthy development.

Whether you realize it or not, you have the power to choose to make your life a success or a failure.

But be doers of the word, and not hearers only, deceiving yourselves.

For if anyone is a hearer of the word and not a doer, he is like a man observing his natural face in a mirror;

for he observes himself, goes away, and immediately forgets what kind of man he was.

James 1:22-24

But we all with unveiled face, beholding as in a mirror the glory of the Lord, are being transformed into the same image from glory to glory, just as by the Spirit of the Lord.

Second Corinthians 3:18

Take Your Self-Image
From The Mirror Of God's Word

Develop the picture of your worth and value from God, not from the false reflections that come out of your past. *Inside of you is everything good that God created you to be — waiting to be released.*

The healing of low self-esteem really hinges on a choice you must make: Will you listen to Satan as he employs all the lies, the distortions, the put-downs, and the hurts of your past to keep you bound by unhealthy, unchristian feelings and concepts about yourself, or will you receive your self-esteem from God and His Word?

Here are six important questions to ask yourself:

1. What right have you to belittle or despise someone whom God loves so deeply?

> In this the love of God was manifested toward us, that God has sent His only begotten Son into the world, that we might live through Him.
>
> First John 4:9

> . . . casting all your care upon Him, for He cares for you.
>
> First Peter 5:7

2. What right have you to belittle or despise someone whom God values so highly?

> For we are His workmanship, created in Christ Jesus for good works, which God prepared beforehand that we should walk in them.
>
> Ephesians 2:10

3. What right have you to belittle or despise someone in whom God delights?

Beloved, I pray that you may prosper in all things and be in health, just as your soul prospers.

Third John 2

4. What right have you to belittle or despise someone whom God has honored so highly?

See what [an incredible] quality of love the Father has given (shown, bestowed on) us, that we should [be permitted to] be named and called and counted the children of God!

First John 3:1 (AMP)

5. What right have you to belittle or despise someone whom God has provided for so fully?

He who did not spare His own Son, but delivered Him up for us all, how shall He not with Him also freely give us all things?

Romans 8:32

6. What right have you to belittle or despise someone whom God has planned for so carefully?

For I know the plans I have for you, declares the Lord, plans to prosper you and not to harm you, plans to give you hope and a future.

Jeremiah 29:11 (NIV)

Begin aligning your image with God's image of you by meditating on how God actually sees you through the mirror of His Word.

Release your image through confession — you must begin speaking God's image and opinion of you!

Seven Things To Affirm Daily

1. I am more than a conqueror in Jesus' name and well able to overcome the problems of life and defeat every attack of the devil. (Romans 8:37)

2. I am recreated in Christ Jesus with the life, nature, ability and wisdom of God within me. (Second Corinthians 5:17)

3. I am the righteousness of God in Christ, and I rule and reign in this life as a king. (Second Corinthians 5:21; Romans 5:17)

4. I belong to God and I am His workmanship, therefore I am free from sickness, poverty, fear, and inferiority. (Ephesians 2:10)

5. The blood of Jesus Christ has cleansed me from all unrighteousness, therefore all sin consciousness, guilt, condemnation, and inferiority are under my feet. (First John 1:9)

6. I stand before the Father, the angels, and demons, and boldly declare that I am worthy to receive all of the blessing and promises of God! (Hebrews 4:16)

7. I am successful in life because God is my source and He prospers the work of my hands. Everything I touch is blessed, and God's favor upon me makes me a blessing everywhere I go. (Isaiah 48:17)

Chapter Four Review

1. The starting point for both success and happiness is a healthy self-image.

2. Nothing can stop you except you — your background, education, circumstances — none of these can hold you back unless *you* let them.

3. Even medical research has shown that we tend to act in harmony with our mental self-portrait.

4. You will never rise, you will never perform, you will never achieve, and you will never attain beyond your level of self-worth.

5. Your mental picture of yourself is the key to your healthy development.

6. Develop the picture of your worth and value from God, not from the false reflections that come out of your past.

7. Begin aligning your image with God's image of you by meditating on how God actually sees you through the mirror of His Word.

Almost always,

attitude makes the difference.

Whether you think you can or can't,

you'll usually be right.

Chapter Five
Seeing Yourself As A Winner

And the Lord will make you the head and not the tail; you shall be above only, and not be beneath, if you heed the commandments of the Lord your God, which I command you today, and are careful to observe them.

Deuteronomy 28:13

HENRY FORD ONCE SAID, "Think you can or think you can't, either way you will be right." As you reach out for success, a vitally important asset you must acquire and maintain is a winner's attitude.

God wants you to have a dream!

God wants you to have a vision!

God wants you to have hope!

God wants the desires of your heart to become a reality!

Literature and history are full of people who suffered from severe handicaps, often had talents that were inferior to those around them, sometimes lived in the worst of circumstances, and usually faced many defeats. Yet many of those people are listed among the winners in life's Hall of Fame. Why? What made them achieve when others around them failed, had greater opportunities, and often had far greater resources?

The secret is this: They had a winners attitude!

Because they saw themselves as winners and not as losers, those who were saddled with disabilities and adversities have managed to overcome them, becoming some of the world's greatest men and women.

Cripple him, and you have a *Sir Walter Scott.*

Lock him in a prison cell, and you have a *John Bunyan.*

Raise him in abject poverty, and you have an *Abraham Lincoln.*

Strike him down with infantile paralysis, and he becomes a *Franklin D. Roosevelt.*

Burn him so severely in a schoolhouse fire that the doctors say he will never walk again, and you have a *Glen Cunningham,* who set the world's record in 1934 for running a mile in four minutes and six seconds.

Deafen a genius composer, and you have a *Ludwig von Beethoven.*

Have him born black in a society filled with racial discrimination and you have a *Martin Luther King, Jr.*

Make him the first child to survive in a poor Italian family of eighteen children, and you have an *Enrico Caruso.*

Call him a slow learner, even retarded, and write him off as illiterate, and you have an *Albert Einstein.*

We cannot always control what others do to us, what happens to us, where we are born, what physical impairments we have, how much money we start out with, what others think of us, what others expect of us, or how high our I.Q. is.

But each of us can and does control how we react to what others do to us, how we cope with what happens to us, how well we use the physical abilities we have, what we do with the resources we have been given, how we respond to the opinions of others, whether we can, or will, live up to other's expectations, and what we do with the I.Q. we have.

> I call heaven and earth as witnesses today against you, that I have set before you life and death, blessing and cursing; therefore choose life, that both you and your descendants may live.

Deuteronomy 30:19

The Choice Is Yours

The first truth you must embrace is that whatever evil, disappointment, or difficulty has occurred in your life, God was, is, and always will be on your side. *Bad* things happen to good people because we live in a fallen world with fallen men making decisions that aren't always God's will. But the Bible says that God is responsible for everything that is *truly good.*

> Every good gift and every perfect gift is from above, and comes down from the Father of lights, with whom there is no variation or shadow of turning.

James 1:17

> This is the message which we have heard of Him and declare to you, that God is light and in Him is no darkness at all.

First John 1:5

When you understand God is the one Who wants you to succeed and be happy in life, you have courage and strength through Jesus Christ to overcome the challenges — past, present, and future — you face. When you understand it is Satan who wants you to fail and be miserable, you have joy and confidence by His Word to exercise the authority given to you in Jesus' name, defeating doubt, unbelief, and fear. You can choose those good things God wants to give you.

41

Choose health!

Choose prosperity!

Choose victory!

Choose abundant life!

Choose success and the blessings of God!

The choice is yours. Make a decision to be everything that God created you to be, despite the obstacles in your path.

Delight yourself also in the Lord, And he shall give you the desires of your heart.

Psalm 37:4

God wants the desires of your heart to become a reality!

God wants you to begin to see the good things He has planned and prepared for your life!

God wants to give you His inspired ideas.

Let me share some success stories with you which are examples of what can happen when you act on God's inspired ideas. These men didn't say, "Oh, that's ridiculous!" They chose to believe that great things come from one tiny idea.

There was a forty-year-old man working for $20 a week. He had an inspired idea to mass produce the automobile. Twenty years later, he was the richest man in the world. His name was *Henry Ford.*

A man sitting on the front porch of his house, watching his cat claw at a canary in a cage, had an inspired idea. He saw a way to get cotton off a seed and invented the cotton gin. His name was *Eli Whitney.*

A man whose talent was knowing color and how to use it to make things beautiful had an inspired idea. He founded a cosmetics business that made him wealthy. It was the Revlon Company. His name was *Charles Revson.*

God created everyone with a single purpose in life — to reach his or her maximum potential and to be everything He created them to be!

You Can Get Inspired Ideas, Too

Researchers say that over 2,000 ideas a day pass through our minds. All we need to do is capture that one sound, God-inspired idea and act on it to see it become a reality.

God will give you creative, inspired ideas, and if you act on them according to His plan, they will successfully come to pass.

Roll your works upon the Lord — commit and trust them wholly to Him; [He will cause your thoughts to become agreeable to His will, and] so shall your plans be established and succeed.

Proverbs 16:3 (AMP)

Most of the limitations that keep us from realizing our full potential in life are artificial, or not the limitation they seem to be. They are imposed on us by circumstances or by other people. Some artificial limitations include:

- our age (we're too old or too young)
- empty pockets
- past failures
- troubles and pains
- the shortsightedness of those around us
- lack of education
- fears
- doubts

Colonel Sanders was "too old" to start a business.

The Wright brothers knew that no one had ever flown.

Florence Chadwick knew that others had died trying to cross the English channel.

Henry Ford faced a "lack of demand" for his automobiles.

David was too young, too unskilled, and too poorly equipped to face Goliath.

Marks Of A Winner

The winners in this world have always been those who have relentlessly chosen to master their circumstances, instead of allowing their circumstances to master them. *How much more should a child of God be a winner!*

Your conversation reveals whether you are a winner or a loser. Losers major on their *problems*. Winners focus on their *possibilities*. Losers discuss their *obstacles*. Winners talk about their *opportunities*.

Losers talk disease. Winners talk about health. Losers talk about the devil's achievements. Winners talk about God's victories. Losers talk like victims. Winners talk like victors. Losers have a slaveship mentality. Winners have a Sonship mentality.

Losers find themselves saying,

"If only I had more money, I could..."

"If only my circumstances were different, I could..."

"If only my race was different, I could..."

"If only I was better educated, I could..."

"If only I had not done..."

While losers make excuses, winners pursue their goals!

Winners:	Losers:
Always have an idea.	Always have an excuse.
Always say, "I'll do it!"	Always say, "It's not my job!"
See an answer for every problem.	See a problem for every answer.
Always say, "I can!"	Always say, "I can't!"
Look for a way to do it.	Look for a way to get out of it.

Almost always, *attitude* makes the difference between being a loser and being a winner. Whether you think you can or can't, you'll usually be right!

Winners compare their achievements with their goals, while losers compare their achievements with those of other people.

Richard Petty has won more prize money than any other stock car driver in the history of the sport. Here is his account of what happened after his very first race:

"Mama!" he shouted as he rushed into the house, "There were thirty-five cars that started, and I came in second in the race!"

"You lost!" his mother replied.

"But Mama!" he protested, "Don't you think it's pretty good to come in second in my first race — especially with so many starters?"

"Richard," she said sternly, "You don't have to run second to anybody!"

Instead of allowing his mother's words to crush his initiative, he took them as a challenge. For the next two decades, Richard Petty dominated stock car racing, and many of his records still stand unbroken.

While losers compare themselves with others, winners compare their achievements with their goals and potential.

Chapter Five Review

1. Henry Ford once said, "Think you can or can't — either way you will be right."

2. As you reach out for success, a vitally important asset you need is a winner's attitude.

3. Some of the world's greatest men and women have been saddled with disabilities and adversities but have managed to overcome them.

4. The choice is yours. Make a decision to be everything that God created you to be.

5. God will give you creative, inspired ideas, and if you act on them according to His plan, they will successfully come to pass.

6. While losers make excuses, winners make their goals!

7. While losers compare themselves with others, winners compare their achievements with their goals and potential.

The success of a man is not measured

by what heights he has risen to, but

by what depths he has climbed from.

Chapter Six
Success Through A Right Attitude

This is the day which the Lord has made; We will rejoice and be glad in it.

Psalms 118:24

Rejoice in the Lord always. Again I will say, rejoice!

Philippians 4:4

. . . the joy of the Lord is your strength.

Nehemiah 8:10

YOUR ATTITUDE CAN make you or break you, heal you or hurt you, make you friends or make you enemies, get you uptight or put you at ease, make you miserable or make you happy, and make you a failure or make you an achiever.

By an act of your will, you can fill your mind with what is positive and as a result lead a successful, happy life. The Bible tells you how to do it.

Fix your thoughts on what is true and good and right. Think about things that are pure and lovely, and dwell on the fine, good things in others. Think about all you can praise God for and be glad about.

Philippians 4:8 (paraphrase)

Your attitude is far more important than anything else, because it will determine whether you are a victim of or a victor over the facts and circumstances in your life, what others say about you, your past, your education, and your finances.

If you give in to negative thoughts, allowing them to dwell within your mind, there is very little chance you will be happy and fulfilled in life. Attitudes like a negative outlook on life, making excuses, wasting time, pettiness, inflexibility, feeling sorry for yourself, procrastination, lack of self-discipline, and bad habits will hold you back from becoming all you were created to be.

On the other hand, a positive attitude like this — "The seeds of greatness are in me! God never created me to be a 'nobody' but a real 'somebody.'" — can put you over anything!

William James said, "The greatest discovery of my generation is that a person can alter his life by altering his attitude of mind."

A hit song written by Johnny Mercer during the Second World War contained the words "accentuate the positive, eliminate the negative."

You must be a positive person to be fulfilled in life.

There are two kinds of people in the world — positive people and negative people. Optimistic, positive persons jump out of bed in the morning and say, "Good morning, Lord!" Pessimistic, negative persons pull the covers up over their heads and moan, "Good Lord, it's morning!" Which kind of person are you?

Whether you are an optimist or a pessimist now, the choice of what you will be in the future is yours, and yours alone. If you are like someone who isn't happy unless they are miserable, you can stay that way. If you want to be joyful, enthusiastic, and excited about life, you can be regardless of your circumstances.

If you choose to be a positive person, you n.
terms with this principle: Put garbage into your .
you're going to produce garbage. Put good thoughts .   .ur
mind, and good actions will follow.

> Don't let the world around you squeeze you into its own
> mold, but let God re-make you so that your whole attitude of
> mind is changed. Thus you will prove in practice that the will
> of God is good, acceptable and perfect.
>
> Romans 12: 2 (J.B. Phillips)

> Jesus said to him, If you can believe, all things are possible
> to him who believes.
>
> Mark 9:23

*Your mind needs to be reconditioned by God's thoughts, so that
you can see the possible in place of the impossible.*

Let me tell you a story that will illustrate what I am saying.
It involves a scientific experiment by a group of researchers
studying the process of conditioning the mind.

In an aquarium, they placed many minnows and one large
pike. A pike is a game fish that thrives on minnow dinners.
Naturally, the pike gobbled up those little minnows and had a
feast for himself.

The scientists then put a pane of glass across the middle of
the aquarium. The pike was contained on one side of the glass,
and minnows were added on the other side. The glass partition
remained in place for several weeks.

The pike would run up to the glass, trying to get to the
minnows, but he would just hit his head, getting nowhere. He
saw the minnows, but he couldn't get to them.

After awhile, the scientists removed the glass. The pike
swam freely all around the minnows, but he didn't eat even one

of them. Why? Because by this time, he had been conditioned by the presence of the glass. It had convinced him he couldn't eat minnows anymore!

Eventually the pike died of starvation, totally surrounded by delicious little minnows. It is the same way with us. We become *conditioned* to lack, sickness, and failure, accepting problems as insurmountable.

Failure is the result of coming under the influence of the world of man instead of the Word of God.

If the pike had stopped going by how things looked, or how he thought they looked, and acquired a higher knowledge, a broader perspective, then he would have devoured a batch of delicious minnows and lived to eat more. Instead, he died of starvation because he refused to change his thinking.

Knowledge is information, and the right kind of information gives us the ability to see things correctly, coming into agreement with God's truth, which is reality.

Renew Your Mind With God's Thinking

Let this mind be in you which was also in Christ Jesus.

Philippians 2:5

Our minds can be released to new accomplishments, new life, and new success, if we renew our minds with God's way of thinking. God does not want us to be crushed by limitation, He wants us to crush them.

God created me in His image for great accomplishments — love, power, victory, prosperity, success, and honor.

You might say, "I can't be a good wife!" "I can't get good grades in school!" "I can't handle this!" "I can't face life any longer!"

Yes, you can! God's Word says that you can do all things through Christ who strengthens you. (See Philippians 4:13).

Right now, wherever you are reading this, I want you to know that the Lord is looking at you, and when you can say "I can," according to His Word, you are determining God's "I cans" to change your situation.

When you start saying, "I can do all things through Christ Who strengthens me," then you are allowing God to work in your situation, because "all things are possible" with God and those who believe. Start speaking the Word of God, which says "I can!" When you do, you'll change your family, your job, and any area where you need help.

Christ will put you over in life if you will start to say, "I can through Him."

I like what John D. Rockefeller said, "A key to success is common people doing common things uncommonly." A believer who relies on the wisdom and power of God to live his life is a common person doing things uncommonly!

Renew Your Strength With God's Strength

Those who press on toward excellence in the kingdom of God must also have a tenacity of will. They must be totally committed and dedicated to be and accomplish all God has created them to be and do. As inspiration, meditate and ponder on the following inspiring nuggets.

Thomas Edison conducted some 10,000 experiments before he finally invented a way to harness electricity for use. He had 10,000 opportunities to say, "I can't do it." And you can be sure that he had "friends" who were telling him, "You can't do it!" But nothing could change his mind. He said, "I can," over 10,000 times!

Frank Woolworth opened the successful Woolworth's chain stores, but he didn't begin as a tycoon. In the beginning, Frank was so dumb and inexperienced that no one would take a chance on hiring him. Finally, he said, "I'll work for free," just to get some experience. He was such an outstanding worker, so exciting in his concepts, that he became a multi-millionaire!

Charles Goodyear imagined a process that would strengthen rubber while increasing its elasticity, to make it suitable for use on wheels. Everyone said "It can't be done!" But after saying "I can," for twenty years, he finally developed a process called vulcanization. Goodyear refused defeat, and we now have rubber tires on our vehicles.

Abraham Lincoln was called a gorilla and a buffoon. He was labeled by one of his peers as an embarrassment to the Republic. I'd tell you who those critics were, but nobody seems to remember *their* names!

Henry Ford failed and went broke five times before he finally succeeded.

Babe Ruth, who is considered by many sports historians to be the greatest athlete of all time, famous for setting the home run record in baseball, also holds the record for strikeouts.

Winston Churchill did not become Prime Minister of England until he was 62, and then only after a lifetime of defeats and setbacks. His greatest contributions came when he was a senior citizen.

Walt Disney went broke seven times and had one nervous breakdown before success smiled on him.

These people succeeded because they persevered, they didn't quit. As a matter of fact, the major difference between the big shot and the little shot is that the big shot is just a little shot who kept shooting!

Disregard and reject every thought, concept, idea, counsel, image, or vision that in any way diminishes, devaluates, demoralizes, depreciates, discredits, or depresses your vision of God's image in you!

A successful insurance executive named Art Miller gave this definition of success: "The success of a man is not measured by what heights he has risen to, but by what depths he has climbed from."

Chapter Six Review

1. By an act of your will, you can fill your mind with what is positive and as a result lead a successful, happy life.

2. If you give in to negative thoughts, allowing them to dwell within your mind, there is little chance of your being happy and fulfilled in life.

3. William James said, "The greatest discovery of my generation is that a person can alter his life by altering his attitude of mind.

4. You must be a positive person to succeed in life.

5. Put garbage into your mind, and you're going to get garbage out. Put good thoughts into your mind, and good actions will come out.

6. Your mind needs to be reconditioned by God's thoughts, so that you can see the possible in place of the impossible.

7. Christ will put you over in life if you will start to say, "*I can in Him.*"

8. The major difference between the big shot and the little shot is that the big shot is just a little shot who kept shooting!

One of the worst crimes

you can commit against yourself

is to play the Comparison Game.

Don't do it! Stop comparing yourself

with other people.

Chapter Seven
You Are Somebody Special

But you are a chosen generation, a royal priesthood, a holy nation, His own special people, that you may proclaim the praises of Him who called you out of darkness into His marvelous light;

who once were not a people but are now the people of God, who had not obtained mercy but now have obtained mercy.

First Peter 2:9,10

Being confident of this very thing, that He who has begun a good work in you will complete it until the day of Jesus Christ.

Philippians 1:6

A YOUNG BOY PUT UP A SIGN in bold letters on his bedroom wall: "I'm me and I'm good 'cause God made me and God don't make junk!"

This boy already had a key to life that many older people never find: he had a positive attitude toward himself. He was saying — "God Made Me Somebody Special ! ! !"

For we are His workmanship, created in Christ Jesus for good works, which God prepared beforehand that we should walk in them.

Ephesians 2:10

God doesn't create cheap merchandise. You are His creation. You have worth. You have value. He implanted in you the seeds of success, faith, and power. Act like it! Live like it!

Stop belittling yourself. Stop saying "I'm stupid, I'm dumb." Do you have the mind of Christ? Then you are superbrilliant! Say aloud, "I have the mind of Christ."

Upon the death of Albert Einstein, the genius physicist who formulated the theory of relativity, scientists analyzed his brain. They discovered he had used approximately ten percent of his thinking capacity. The average person uses somewhere between six and eight percent of his mind's unlimited capacity.

Just think, it took only a little bit of extra effort on the part of Einstein — tiny bit more extra mental effort — to produce his brilliant theories. Ideas no one else had thought about before came from his mind.

Just as He did with Einstein, God created you with a brain and a mind that has the ability to think and choose its thoughts. He enabled your mind to exercise will power. He created your mind for accomplishment, success, and brilliance.

God didn't make Einstein better than He made you.

Someone special — that's you! God made you unique. There is no one else just like you. In the master plan of God, all men are created with many things in common. Yet each is distinct and different from any other human being.

No two snowflakes are identical. Each blade of grass is different from all the others. How much greater are you than a snowflake, than a blade of grass? Of all the billions of people created, there is no one else who has ever lived or who is alive now that is just like you. *You are a divine original.*

You are, in many ways, unique. That is, you are the only one of your kind. You have unique talents and abilities, unique opportunities, unique mental powers, a unique personality, and a unique self-image.

The fact is, no one can do exactly what you can do exactly as you can do it, no one has exactly the same opportunities you have, no one knows exactly what you know, no one has a personality exactly like yours, and no one sees you exactly as you see yourself.

I want you to discover through God's Word what a wonderful person you really are and can become, no matter what has happened in your life, no matter what you have done or failed to do, and no matter how you think of yourself at this moment.

Loving Yourself Is Not A Sin — It's A Commandment!

And you shall love the Lord your God with all your heart, with all your soul, with all your mind, and with all your strength.' This is the first commandment.

And the second like it, is this: You shall love your neighbor as yourself. There is no other commandment greater than these.

Mark 12:30,31

Notice Jesus' teaching on self-love. To love yourself is the Christian thing to do!

To love yourself is not only the healthy and decent thing to do, the way to be liberated from negative attitudes, and the way to be free to love others and respect what God respects. To love yourself is to do what Jesus told you to do.

It is easy to love and value yourself when you understand how God sees you in Christ. You are a *new creation* in Christ, not a repair job! You are not renovated like an old building or reconditioned like old furniture.

Stop condemning yourself for past sins and telling others your faults. Receive God's forgiveness and forgive yourself. You are loved and accepted by God, so love and accept yourself.

In Christ — you are God's workmanship!

In Christ — you are valuable and precious!

In Christ — you are significant and special!

In Christ — you are a somebody, not a nobody!

In Christ — there is no condemnation!

In Christ — you are forgiven!

See yourself through God's eyes.

Recognize your value — you are God's best. You were created for power and prosperity, for success and honor. You were built to be blessed and to be a blessing. You were created in the image of God!

God made you first class. There is nothing inferior about God or His workmanship!

Accept the value that God has placed on you ! ! !

Say these ten positive Bible-based affirmations aloud:

- *God is my source!*
- *God is stronger than the strongest!*
- *God has a good plan for my life!*
- *God will bring good out of this bad situation!*
- *God forgives me!*
- *God is with me!*
- *Nothing is impossible with God!*
- *God is bigger than any problem facing me!*
- *God is good, God is big, and God is in control!*
- *God loves me — He really loves me!*

In God's sight you are not a wash-out, a complete failure, or a hopeless case. God says you are worth loving, so begin to love yourself. God's greatest creation is *you!*

Looking To Jesus

For we dare not class ourselves or compare ourselves with those who commend themselves. But they, measuring themselves by themselves, and comparing themselves among themselves, are not wise.

Second Corinthians 10:12

One of the worst crimes you can commit against yourself is to play the Comparison Game, which will destroy your awareness of being God's unique and beloved creation. Don't compare yourself with another person. It is not God's will for you. It is an unhealthy thing to do.

You need to get it through your head that you were never made to be like any other person. Accept yourself for who you are, and with God's help become that wonderful person He created you to be. Refuse to play the Comparison Game, and you will be a healthier, happier person.

The only mirror believers should ever look into to see themselves is the Word of God. Instead of being sin-conscious, or concentrating on every transgression, defeat, and failure, and comparing ourselves to those around us, we should become son-conscious, concentrating on our Lord and who we are in Him.

Looking unto Jesus, the author and finisher of our faith.

Hebrews 12:2

Almost sixty years ago, E. W. Kenyon penned these inspiring words:

"Stepping out of sin-consciousness into son-consciousness is stepping out of failure into success. It means stepping out of that inferiority complex that has held us prisoners for years.

"It means becoming the person you have dreamed about.

"Do you remember the picture in the magazine of the little scrawny fellow sitting by the side of a great, big, strong, muscular man, seeing the big man take his girl away from him? Then the little scrawny man goes into the gymnasium and develops his muscles until they are strong. Then he goes out and faces other men unafraid.

"You go into God's gymnasium and come in contact with the great gymnastic teacher of spiritual things. You let Him put you through a course until you stand in front of the world complete in all His finished work, until your inferiority has been swallowed up in His dominant, victorious Spirit, until you whisper, 'Greater is He that is in me, than he that is in the world,' or 'than the doubts and fears that worked in me in the past.'

"I have a Master now Who is building me up instead of the master who kept me in bondage, who kept me down.

"I walked in failure for years. I walked with the sense of my lack of ability and righteousness; but now I walk with Him.

"We are linked together. I am breathing in the courage of His tremendous personality. I am filled with His ability.

"I say, "Good-bye," to the dark, unhappy days of the past. A curtain falls between them and me. I stand now upon the highlands, a victor.

"No longer am I worrying about the lack of money. Lack of money does not lord it over me.

"Lack of ability does not lord it over me now. Lack of opportunity no longer lords it over me. I am not intimidated by circumstances, or filled with fear that I cannot do the work or put it over.

"I know that the Mighty One has taken me over and is putting me over in life since I stepped out of sin-consciousness into son-consciousness."

Therefore, if anyone is in Christ, he is a new creation; old things have passed away; behold, all things have become new.

Second Corinthians 5:17

Chapter Seven Review

1. God does not create cheap merchandise. You are *His* creation.

2. Someone special — that's you. God made you unique. There is no one else just like you. You are a divine original.

3. You are loved and accepted by God, so love and accept yourself!

4. God made you first class! Accept His opinion of you.

5. Don't compare yourself with another person, or you will destroy your awareness of being God's unique and beloved creation.

6. Look to Jesus, Who will put you over in life!

We must never forget or lose sight of who we are in Christ and our abilities in Him, otherwise we will never rise above the restricting natural conditions around us.

Chapter Eight
Accepting God's Opinion Of You

For God has not given us a spirit of fear, but of power and
of love and of a sound mind.

Second Timothy 1:7

But of Him you are in Christ Jesus, who became for us
wisdom from God — and righteousness and sanctification and
redemption.

First Corinthians 1:30

For the law of the Spirit of life in Christ Jesus has made me
free from the law of sin and death.

Romans 8:2

CAN A HEALTHIER SELF-IMAGE be developed? At this
point some of you may be saying, "Oh boy, did I ever get a
bad foundation! No wonder I've got such problems."

The good news is that your self-portrait is not permanently
affixed in place, like a photo encased in plastic in your wallet.
You can change it. You can develop a more accurate and healthy
view of yourself based on the Word of God!

Self-image has been defined as "what *we* think and feel
ourselves to be." But in reality, a healthy self-image, the only
self-image that cannot crumble under any kind of pressure, is

seeing ourselves as *God* sees us — being committed to the truth of His estimation of us — and letting that be how we think and feel about ourselves. Paul referred to his own self-image when he wrote, "By the grace of God I am what I am" First Corinthians 15:10.

So often, one's attitudes are developed and decisions are made based upon wrong assumptions or misinformation. We can base our self-image on what we *think* God thinks about us, and not on what He *actually thinks* about us, which is revealed in His Word.

What Scripture has to say about you is the starting place for developing a healthy, positive, and lasting self-image. This is the self-image God gives to you.

1. God sees you as a new creation in Christ.

Therefore, if anyone is in Christ, he is a new creation; old things have passed away; behold, all things have become new.

Second Corinthians 5:17

You are a brand new species in Christ, a *new creation* in Christ! You have been miraculously born again — given a new spirit — by a supernatural God, and you have received His supernatural life. *Stop identifying with the old you!*

The new birth has placed you in a supernatural dimension, with the ability to overcome the natural conditions of this life! You are not *mere men.* You have *the ability of God!*

As a new creature, you have the Holy Spirit living inside, so how can you fail? The life, nature, substance, and creative ability of God has been imparted to you as a new creation — and God never made a failure yet! You are a son of God, born of God, with the life and nature of God in you.

You're a superman species.

God's life is in your life.

God's nature is your nature.

God's ability is your ability.

God's strength is your strength!

How can you confess lack of ability, weakness, or failure when He is the vine and you are the branch! By faith, draw on that supernatural, life-giving sap!

2. *God sees you righteous in Christ.*

For He made Him who knew no sin to be sin for us, that we might become the righteousness of God in Him.

Second Corinthians 5:21

Even the righteousness of God which is through faith in Jesus Christ to all and on all who believe. For there is no difference.

Romans 3:22

Jesus *became* sin that you might *become* righteous. From the moment you surrender your life to Him, the Father sees you as righteous as His Son, Jesus Christ. Outwardly, you may sin from time to time, but inwardly, in your spirit, where the Holy Spirit dwells, you are righteous.

If you should sin in thought or deed (soul and body), First John 1:9 tells you to repent, and God will forgive you and cleanse your soul from all unrighteousness. *Fellowship* (your daily walk) with Him is restored and remains pure.

But your *relationship* as Father and child, although it began with your decision to accept Jesus as your Lord and Savior, remains secure *solely* through the shed blood of Jesus, *not* by your good deeds. God sees you righteous not by your works, but by the work of Jesus on the cross and at His resurrection.

3. *God sees you as His child.*

But as many as received Him, to them He gave the right to become children of God, even to those who believe in His name.

John 1:12

You are a child of God, born of the Spirit of God, with the life and nature of God in you. God is your spiritual Father!

The children of the devil have the nature of the devil and act like the devil. Likewise, the children of God have the life, nature, and attributes of God, and ought to act like God!

Therefore be imitators of God — copy Him and follow His example — as well-beloved children [imitate their father].

Ephesians 5:1 (AMP)

By birth and by nature you have God's attributes and His abilities — like Father, like son! All that you do must be directed and guided by Him through His instructions for successful living, which are given in the Bible.

4. *God sees you as a joint heir with Jesus.*

And if children, then heirs — heirs of God and joint heirs with Christ.

Romans 8:17

Everything that Jesus has belongs to us as a new creation in Him. We have an inheritance, bought and paid for by His shed blood. By God's grace, in Christ we have become His joint heir.

Being a joint heir with Jesus means we have been redeemed out of everything that pertains to death and the kingdom of darkness, into all that pertains to life and divine prosperity. But in order to obtain the benefits in this life, we must study and find out about them (Ephesians 1:17-19). We have to have knowledge to be able to obtain it (Colossians 1:9-13). One of these benefits is a godly self-image!

5. *God sees you as a king and as a priest.*

For if, because of one man's trespass (lapse, offense) death reigned through that one, much more surely will those who receive [God's] overflowing grace (unmerited favor) and the free gift of righteousness (putting them into right standing with Himself) *reign as kings in life through the One,* Jesus Christ, the Messiah, the Anointed One.

Romans 5:17 (AMP)

And from Jesus Christ, the faithful witness, the first-born from the dead, and the ruler over the kings of the earth. To Him who loved us and washed us from our sins in His own blood,

and *has made us kings and priests to His God and Father,* to Him be glory and dominion for ever and ever. Amen.

Revelation 1:5,6

We are kings and priests in Christ Jesus, blessed with royal authority and the right to minister unto the Lord in praise and worship.

As kings, believers are to rule and reign, which means they have authority, lordship, rulership, and dominion over the situations of life. Dominion means "the right and the power to govern and control."

Which He will manifest in His own time, He who is the blessed and only Potentate, the King of kings and Lord of lords.

First Timothy 6:15

Jesus is the King of kings — we are the kings.
Jesus is the Lord of lords — we are the lords.

For the word of a king is authority and power, and who can say to him, What are you doing?

Ecclesiastes 8:4 (AMP)

We are to exercise dominion in the earth over life's problems, and we do that through the words we speak. When you speak God's Word, you are releasing the power of the Holy Spirit in accordance with His spiritual laws. You can maintain a positive confession of faith in the face of every adversity, because His spirit forces are causing natural conditions to get in line with His Word. When you speak God's Word, you release His creative ability.

Let us therefore come boldly to the throne of grace, that we may obtain mercy and find grace to help in time of need.

Hebrews 4:16

As a priest in Christ, you can walk confidently into the Holy of Holies and make your needs known to God. You have Almighty God's permission to stand in His presence and talk with Him, intercede for others, and receive His strength, wisdom, and direction for your life and the lives of others.

6. *God sees you blessed, prosperous, and healthy.*

Blessed be the God and Father of our Lord Jesus Christ, who has blessed us with every spiritual blessing in the heavenly places in Christ.

Ephesians 1:3

Beloved, I pray that you may prosper in all things and be in health, just as your soul prospers.

Third John 2

In Christ, you have divine ability to be successful and prosperous in every area of life.

I have strength for all things in Christ Who empowers me — I am ready for anything and equal to anything through Him Who infuses inner strength into me, [that is, I am self-sufficient in Christ's sufficiency].

Philippians 4:13 (AMP)

For you know the grace of our Lord Jesus Christ, that though He was rich, yet for your sakes He became poor, that you through His poverty might become rich.

Second Corinthians 8:9

I have come that they may have life, and that they may have it more abundantly.

John 10:10

Abundant life means receiving the very breath of God — you are alive in God. It is a result of the new birth. Receiving God's salvation is your birthright to abundance.

Abundant life means receiving eternal life (*zoe*, the God kind of life). This means a life superior in quality and super-abundant in quantity! To be saved means you are redeemed, restored, made whole, healed, blessed, accepted, uplifted, loved, delivered, victorious, prosperous, and successful.

He who did not spare His own Son, but delivered Him up for us all, how shall He not with Him also freely give us all things?

Romans 8:32

Everything you need to live blessed in this life is provided for you in Christ!

7. *God sees you as more than a conqueror.*

Yet in all these things we are more than conquerors through Him who loved us.

Romans 8:37

> But thanks be to God, Who gives us the victory — making us conquerors — through our Lord Jesus Christ.
>
> First Corinthians 15:57 (AMP)

In Christ, you are more than a conqueror, well able to overcome the problems of life. But you must never forget or lose sight of who you are in Christ and your abilities in Him; otherwise, you will never rise above the restricting natural conditions around you.

As a new creation, your body is the temple of the Holy Spirit, and with the greater one living in you, the devil and all demon forces are under your feet.

> Little children, you are of God — you belong to Him — and have [already] defeated and overcome them [the agents of antichrist], because He Who lives in you is greater (mightier) than he who is in the world.
>
> First John 4:4 (AMP)

> And what agreement has the temple of God with idols? For you are the temple of the living God. As God has said: "I will dwell in them And walk among them. I will be their God and they shall be My people."
>
> Second Corinthians 6:16

Because of Jesus' victory over Satan and Christ living in you, you can defeat all demon spirits, and all the works of the devil are under your feet.

Living a successful Christian life is not your *responsibility*, but your *response* to being in Christ. It is *Christ in us* making us successful.

Know who you are in Christ.

Know Who is inside of you.

Know Who is constantly with you.

What you believe, think, and see yourself to be will determine the quality of your life.

Chapter Eight Review

1. A healthy self-image is seeing yourself as God sees you.

2. A healthy self-image is being committed to the truth of God's estimation of you.

3. God sees you as a new creation in Christ.

4. God sees you as righteous in Christ.

5. God sees you as a born-again child of God.

6. God sees you as a joint heir with Jesus.

7. God sees you as a king and a priest.

8. God sees you as more than a conqueror.

9. God sees you blessed, prosperous, and healthy.

10. In Christ you have divine ability to be successful and prosperous in every area of life.

11. What you believe, think, and see yourself to be will determine the quality of your life.

*God created you **unique***

with the intention that you would

be the best you, you could be.

Chapter Nine
Improving Your Self-Image

Brethren, I do not count myself to have apprehended; but one thing I do, forgetting those things which are behind and reaching forward to those things which are ahead, I press toward the goal for the prize of the upward call of God in Christ Jesus.

Philippians 3:13,14

IT BEARS REPEATING that the Bible says in several places that we should possess a healthy, scriptural self-love. (See Mark 12:30,31 and Ephesians 5:28,29).

Some Christians find it difficult to accept the fact that God desires us to love ourselves. They view self-love as a subtle form of pride or self-adoration. But when we speak of self-love, we are not referring to a self-centered, egotistical love. This form of self-love is *selfish* love.

Having a godly self-love is *not* bragging about your abilities and accomplishments, putting down the abilities or accomplishments of others, exaggerating your abilities or deeds, or out-talking everybody else to get your way. A better word for these practices is arrogance.

Other words which may come to mind are conceit, self-centeredness, and egotism. You can bet your bottom dollar that people who are always bragging, putting others down, exaggerating, or dominating conversations are only trying to bolster their own sagging self-esteem.

A healthy, positive self-image is not self-centered egotism! Someone has said, "The smallest package in the world is a person all wrapped up in himself." In fact, if you want a formula for becoming miserable, the first ingredient is to think only of yourself. Mental depression reigns when someone feels they are the most important person in the world.

People who have a biblical self-love don't look down their noses at others who don't have the advantages they have, or who don't achieve the status and recognition they do. One of the oldest mistakes of people with low self-esteem is the belief that they can elevate themselves by tearing others down. *Godly self-love* simply means we see ourselves as worthwhile creatures *in Christ.*

> But you are a chosen generation, a royal priesthood, a holy nation, His own special people, that you may proclaim the praises of Him who called you out of darkness into His marvelous light;
>
> who once were not a people but are now the people of God, who had not obtained mercy but now have obtained mercy.
>
> First Peter 2:9,10

We see ourselves as valued and loved by God. We see ourselves as creatures bearing the divine image of dignity and honor. Our self-love is based upon a realistic appraisal of our standing as gifted and useful members of the Body of Christ. (See First Corinthians 12:12-24).

Man's Three Basic Emotional Needs

There are three major factors that influence or affect your self-image.

1. *Your sense of belonging.*

The need to be wanted, needed, liked, and enjoyed. You desire people to enjoy you and enjoy your company.

2. *Your sense of worthiness.*

The need to feel good about yourself. A feeling of I am all right! I count! I am part of the plan! I have value!

3. *Your sense of competence.*

A sense of feeling you have achieved. I can do it! I have the ability! I am an achiever in life!

Self-Image Analysis — Where Are You?

These points describe those who have a healthy self-image. As you read through them, take a good, honest look at yourself. Which statements best describe you?

- They feel good about themselves, they feel worthwhile.
- They like themselves and accept both their positive qualities and their weaknesses.
- They are confident, yet realistic.
- They can handle other people's reactions and opinions, both positive and negative.
- They are not afraid to get involved. They set out to accomplish what they are capable of doing and feel others will respond to them.

The following points describe those who have a *poor self-image.* Do any of them describe you?

- They feel unworthy, useless, insignificant, and perhaps despise and hate themselves.

- They do not trust themselves, and they are wary of sharing their ideas with other people, fearing rejection and criticism.

- A major controlling influence in their life is fear — fear of failure, fear of ridicule, fear of rejection, and fear of criticism!

- They are usually preoccupied with their own problems. All they think and talk about are their problems.

- They have a bad attitude toward themselves, and they believe others feel the same toward them.

- In conversation and relationships with other people, they are always on the defensive rather than being open. When you talk to them or try and give them some advice, they react defensively and try to justify their actions, rather than being open. Instead of considering constructive criticism, they will not accept correction, and they will not change. They feel so terrible about themselves, they don't want to hear any correction.

- They never enter into positive relationships with others, because they always feel inferior to other people.

- They constantly label themselves negatively, indulging in self-criticism. "I'm so stupid. I didn't deserve that promotion. I don't have the ability to succeed. I'm dumb. I'm lazy. I'll never be able to do it!"

Change Your Mind!

If you will change the way you *think* about yourself, then your *inward image* will be changed. When you begin to renew your mind and reprogram your thought life with faith-building scriptures about God's opinion of you, then your self-worth, self-concept, self-value, self-esteem, and self-image is affected positively. *You will begin to love yourself because you realize you are divinely loved.*

> **In Whom, because of our faith in Him, we dare to have the boldness, (courage and confidence) of free access — an unreserved approach to God with freedom and without fear.**
>
> **Ephesians 3:12 (AMP)**

This scripture is the *opposite* of a person who has a poor self-image and an inferiority complex. In fact, this scripture shows us a picture of a believer with a healthy self-image, who *recognizes his roots in Christ!*

> **Yet now has [Christ the Messiah,] reconciled [you to God] in the body of His flesh through death, in order to present you holy and faultless and irreproachable in His [the Father's] presence.**
>
> **Colossians 1:22 (AMP)**

You are now a new creation in Christ, and God sees you in Christ — faultless, blameless, and holy! Therefore, it is time to turn your flaws and faults over to Him. Begin to see them as they are — crucified on Jesus' cross. You are no longer a slave to sin and failure. Through Jesus, you can defeat sin and overcome failure. You can be healed of all the wounds of life and go on to fulfill your divine purpose.

Read Second Corinthians 3:4-6. These verses tell you that your ability is God's ability in you, your sufficiency is of God, God has made you worthy and an able minister of the New Covenant! *You are not inadequate in Christ.*

Knowing God loves you is the foundation for a successful relationship with God and a healthy relationship with yourself. His love, which grows stronger and more real as you pursue your relationship with Him, encourages you to have faith, hope, and to love others as He loves you.

> **But we all, with unveiled face, beholding as in a mirror the glory of the Lord, are being transformed into the same image from glory to glory, just as by the Spirit of the Lord!**
>
> **Second Corinthians 3:18**

God accepts you!

God loves you!

God sees you as valuable and precious!

God sees you as somebody special!

Trust God's opinion of you!

You are a child of the Most High God, and God created you with special gifts, special talents, and special abilities. But the decision is yours.

You can choose to identify with the old person you used to be, or you can change your mind to identify with the fact that you are a *new creation in Christ.*

Beware of the following hindrances to a healthy self-image:

- Putting yourself down continually, the habit of self-depreciation, constantly criticizing yourself, advertising your weaknesses, inabilities, and limitations.

- Comparing yourself to others, competitive attitude that causes you to compare your own worst features to someone else's best features.

- Yielding to the spirit of fear (of failure and rejection).

- Dwelling on memories of past failures, mistakes, and negative experiences.

- Obesity, addiction to food.

- Ungodly friendships and associations.

Keys To Developing
Your God-Given Self-Image

1. Start to see yourself, think about yourself, and talk about yourself the way God does.

Therefore, if anyone is in Christ, he is a new creation; old things have passed away; behold, all things have become new.

Second Corinthians 5:17

For we are His workmanship, created in Christ Jesus for good works, which God prepared beforehand that we should walk in them.

Ephesians 2:10

Read, meditate, study, believe, and *affirm* the new creation truths of the New Testament epistles. Take a red pen and mark the scriptures with faith-building statements such as, "in Him", "In Christ," and "In Whom" — *they appear 150 times.*

These new creation "in Him" realities are what you should be feeding on. As you build these truths into your life, you will be building a strong scriptural self-image. You will soon develop a strong righteousness-consciousness, which will eliminate sin-consciousness, guilt, and condemnation.

Persons with an inadequate self-image look primarily to others' praises or criticisms as determining factors in how they feel or think about themselves at a particular moment. Persons with a poor sense of self-worth are slaves to the opinions of others. They are not free to be themselves.

However, a believer with a healthy self-image can carefully consider the instruction and reproof of their elders in the Lord, according to Hebrews 13:7,17. Their identity and value is found in Christ, so they can humbly submit to those in authority over them, while never losing their freedom.

Concentrate and meditate on God's grace, who you are in Christ, His love and acceptance. Remember: nobody can make you feel inferior without *your* permission!

2. *Disconnect yourself from memories of past failures, past mistakes, past sins, and past negative experiences.*

> . . . but one thing I do, forgetting those things which are behind . . . .
>
> **Philippians 3:13**

Many individuals quietly suffer from longstanding guilt and feelings of deep remorse over their past mistakes. When we dwell upon our former shortcomings, we unconsciously destroy the godly self image the Holy Spirit desires us to have.

Poor self-esteem is often the result of failing to alleviate the burden of guilt. Feelings of unresolved guilt can gradually create a sense of failure, frustration, inadequacy, self-condemnation, and self-disappointment.

If this is the case, we must appropriate the cleansing power of forgiveness, which Jesus Christ paid for by the shedding of His blood. (See Ephesians 1:7; First John 1:7,9). This is what the Bible says God does with our sins when we repent:

- He cleanses them white as snow
  Isaiah 1:18; Psalm 51:7

- He removes them as far as the east is from the west
  Psalm 103:12

* He casts them behind His back
  Isaiah 38:17

- He blots them out
  Isaiah 43:25

- He remembers them no more
  Hebrews 10:17

- He casts them into the depths of the sea
  Micah 7:19

- He forgives us and cleanses us by the blood of Christ
  First John 1:7,9.

When you fail, admit or confess it to God, your Father, and then refuse to condemn yourself (Romans 8:1). Remember, you are in the process of becoming like Christ, and spiritual growth takes time!

If God has forgiven you, then forgive yourself. If God no longer condemns you, then stop condemning yourself. If God has wiped the slate clean and has forgotten your sinful past, then you forget about it!

3. Do not compare yourself with other people.

For we dare not class ourselves or compare ourselves with those who commend themselves. But they, measuring themselves by themselves, and comparing themselves among themselves, are not wise.

Second Corinthians 10:12

You are a unique person, and God loves you just as you are, so accept yourself the way He does. God enjoys you in your uniqueness, so have the same attitude toward yourself. The Bible says this is a wise thing to do!

But now God has set the members, each one of them, in the body just as he pleased.

And the eye cannot say to the hand, "I have no need of you."

Now you are the body of Christ, and members individually.

First Corinthians 12:18,21,27

Avoid the trap of making carnal comparisons. Start helping others to see themselves as God sees them by accepting them, loving them, and encouraging them. Give them the dignity they deserve as one of God's unique human creatures.

4. Become an ambassador of good words, guard your tongue and watch what you say about yourself.

Death and life are in the power of the tongue, And those who love it will eat its fruit.

Proverbs 18:21

You don't like it much when someone puts you down, do you? You especially don't like negative comments when they are false, or only half true, right? Yet one word of self-criticism does more damage to your self-esteem as a word of criticism from someone else!

People who continuously say bad things about themselves eventually come to believe what they say. Once they believe themselves, they act on their beliefs. They become the "nowhere people" that they have told themselves they are.

Do not label yourself negatively ("I am clumsy," and so on). You tend to become the label you give yourself. Stop advertising your mistakes and limitations.

Watch your words, as they are spiritual forces. Your words are spiritual containers of life or death.

Here are some common negative labels people often give themselves:

- I'm no good!
- I'm a failure!
- I'll never get a promotion!
- I can't do this or that!
- No one loves me!

- I can never do anything right!
- I always lose!
- I'm not important!
- I'm insignificant!
- Nothing ever works out for me!

Negative labels brainwash your mind. They form a mental picture of your inabilities, insecurities, and failures! Destroy all negative labels with *sciptural mind* and *mouth* programming. Always speak words of life and faith over yourself. Learn to value yourself!

> I have strength for all things in Christ Who empowers me — I am ready for anything and equal to anything through Him who infuses inner strength into me, [that is, I am self-sufficient in Christ's sufficiency].
>
> Philippians 4:13 (AMP)

5. Select wise friendships and associate with people who build you up and contribute to your faith.

> Do not be misled: "Bad company corrupts good character."
>
> First Corinthians 15:33 (NIV)

> He who walks with wise men will be wise, But the companion of fools will be destroyed.
>
> Proverbs 13:20

People *do* affect our outlook. For example, once a man was about to jump off a high bridge and commit suicide. Another man came along, and the two sat down to talk. After about an hour, both of them jumped off the bridge.

In fact, many people conspire to give us a negative outlook on life. The nature of news reporting is such that we hear much more about the bad than the good. We always hear about the plane that crashes, not about the thousands of planes that land safely. Even weather reporters warn us of a ten percent chance of rain, instead of a ninety percent chance of a beautiful day!

When you spend time with successful Christians, they reinforce your biblical attitudes about life. Believers who humbly respect themselves and their abilities in Christ will help you feel good about yourself and your abilities as a child of God.

A successful believer may have thousands of *acquaintances,* but only a handful of *friends.* Spend your time with believers from whom you can draw strength and to whom you can give strength. True friends can do wonders for your godly self-esteem! "A friend is someone who knows all about you, and loves you anyway," someone has wisely said.

Deliberately associate with people who are strong in Christ-like character, who look on the bright side of life. (See Hebrews 13:7). Pick out those people who are optimistic and excited about life, and I'll guarantee you some of it will rub off on you. The benefits of their friendship will be enormous.

You acquire much of your thinking, mannerisms, and characteristics from the people you are around. This is true whether the people you associate with are good or bad. When you associate with the "right" people, who have a positive, successful, victorious "in Christ" outlook on life, you greatly enhance your chances of winning and being a winner!

6. *Walk uprightly before God and live a life of honesty, integrity, and holiness.*

... in all things showing yourself to be a pattern of good works; in doctrine showing integrity, reverence, incorruptibility,

For the grace of God that brings salvation has appeared to all men, teaching us that, denying ungodliness and worldly lusts, we should live soberly, righteously and godly in the present age.

Titus 2:7,11,12

For the Lord God is a sun and a shield; The Lord will give grace and glory; No good thing will He withhold From those who walk uprightly.

Psalms 84:11

Our ability to prosper depends upon the amount of God's truth and wisdom we know, exercise, and apply to our lives. The Bible is the source book of that truth and wisdom, holding the keys to our success in life.

Don't engage in any activity forbidden in the Bible. Don't continue to do anything you know is of no value to you and your growth in Christ. Cut out any relationships harmful to your spiritual life in Christ, and do not participate in anything that could become an addicting or a destructive habit. Do what is right and pleasing in the eyes of God!

7. Stay positive in your thought life, and protect yourself from all negative, destructive influences.

Finally, brethren, whatever things are true, whatever things are noble, whatever things are just, whatever things are pure, whatever things are lovely, whatever things are of good report, if there is any virtue and if there is anything praiseworthy — meditate on these things.

Philippians 4:8

You will keep him in perfect peace, Whose mind is stayed on You.

Isaiah 26:3

Guard what you watch, read, and listen to. Remember, *you* control your environment, TV, radio, magazines, books, home videos. To build a healthy self-image, you must avoid some things, because everything that goes into your mind has an effect and is permanently recorded. It either builds and prepares you for the future or it tears you down and reduces your accomplishment possibilities for the future.

> . . . bringing every thought into captivity to the obedience of Christ.
>
> Second Corinthians 10:5

Discipline your negative thoughts by submitting them to the positive reality of God's Word. The Scriptures remind us to set our mind on those things which are true, honest, just, pure, lovely, and of good report. (See Philippians 4:8).

We must guard our thought life.

Your mind can be your worst enemy, or a good friend. Your thoughts can either build godly self-esteem or undermine your godly sense of self-worth. If you continually yield to corrupt thinking, or indulge in negative confessions about yourself, you will inevitably destroy your self-esteem.

We all know people who create a negative atmosphere wherever they go. Why? Because they like to talk about everything and everyone in a negative way. Watch this and see if it is not true. Every time you talk negatively about another human being, you infect the atmosphere with bad feelings. So don't criticize or condemn people, and don't spend time with those who do.

Mentally rehearse the victories and successes God brought in the past. Replay the times you tasted victory in times of trouble through the delivering hand of the Lord. Look at your achievements through Christ.

> For as he thinks in his heart, so is he.
>
> Proverbs 23:7

Chapter Nine Review

1. Godly self-love simply means that we see ourselves as worthwhile creatures in Christ.

2. God created you unique with the intention that you would be the best you, you can be!

3. You are now a new creation in Christ and God sees you faultless, blameless, and holy!

4. The attitude and image that we portray to other people is a reflection of the mental portrait hanging on the wall of our minds.

5. You are a child of the Most High God, and God created you with special gifts, special talents, and special abilities!

6. Start to see yourself, think about yourself, and talk about yourself the way God does.

7. Disconnect yourself from memories of past failures, past mistakes, past sins, and past negative experiences.

8. Do not compare yourself with other people.

9. Become an ambassador of good words, guard your tongue and watch what you say about yourself.

10. Select wise friendships, and associate with people who build you up and contribute to your faith.

11. Walk uprightly before God, and live a life of honesty, integrity, and holiness.

12. Stay positive in your thought life, and protect yourself from all negative, destructive influences.

13. Don't criticize or condemn people, and don't spend time with those who do.

You need to take the Bible

and begin developing through

the Scriptures a successful,

overcomer's image of yourself.

Chapter Ten
Putting Yourself In The Way Of Success

In everything you do, put God first, and he will direct you and crown your efforts with success.

Proverbs 3:6 (TLB)

This Book of the Law shall not depart from your mouth, but you shall meditate in it day and night, that you may observe to do according to all that is written in it. For then you will make your way prosperous, and then you will have good success.

Joshua 1:8

"For I know the plans I have for you," declares the Lord, "plans to prosper you and not to harm you, plans to give you hope and a future."

Jeremiah 29:11 (NIV)

A LOT OF CHRISTIANS TODAY are emphasizing the importance of being a success, a winner. That, too, can lead to pride when the emphasis is on the goal or end result and not on the source of success, Jesus Christ.

Without an emphasis on the phrase "through Christ," the teaching that Christians should be winners can foster pride.

With this phrase, however, it can foster a healthy self-image and walk of faith to the glory of God.

Our success only comes through Christ!

Mark, chapter 4, teaches that your heart is like the soil of the earth, and it is designed to produce whatever you sow or plant into it, the Word of God or the lies of Satan.

Keep your heart with all vigilance and above all that you guard, for out of it flow the springs of life.

Proverbs 4:23 (AMP)

Until you really believe you *can,* you *can't.* What you have as an *inward image* inside you will determine the direction and prosperity of your life on the *outside. Unscriptural images produce negative results!*

There is a spiritual law of attraction. By your attitude, words, and actions, you attract prosperity or lack, victory or defeat, success or failure. Here are some negative attitudes that hinder the believer:

We are always struggling financially.

I'll never get a promotion in my company.

I can't seem to do anything right.

Nobody likes me.

Our children won't listen to us.

Nothing good ever happens to me.

Things are bad and getting worse.

But if your eye is bad, your whole body will be full of darkness. If therefore the light that is in you is darkness, how great is that darkness!

Matthew 6:23

"If your eye is bad" means you are not thinking according to the Word of God. Your perspective is incorrect, and you are living in darkness. You always look for the worst. You see sickness instead of health, bad instead of good, lack instead of plenty, fear and discouragement instead of faith and encouragement, hate instead of love, jealousy and strife instead of harmony in relationships, and no opportunities instead of opportunities.

To have an evil eye also means that negative situations and things hold your attention rather than the Word of God. However, by continually seeing things correctly on the *inside,* this will produce things correctly on the *outside.* You have to stop seeing the problems and start seeing the solutions God has already provided.

You can agree with faith instead of unbelief, health instead of sickness, prosperity instead of poverty, victory instead of defeat, the joy of the Lord instead of depression. You do this by immersing your thoughts in what the Bible says, agreeing with what God says, declaring that God's Word will prevail over the circumstances and challenges in your life.

Meditation in God's Word — The Key To Victory And Joy

We tend to hope that circumstances will change to make us happier! That's why we say:

If only the economy would improve.

If only interest rates were not so high.

If only I could find a better job.

If only I could sell my house.

If only I could lose weight.

If only I could take a holiday for a few weeks.

Do not concern yourself with the outward circumstances. Instead, work on changing your *inward* image.

You have to change inwardly, because inferiority, fear of failure, insecurity, self-esteem, peace of mind, stability, etc. have nothing to do with *outward* circumstances, but they have to do with your *internal* condition.

Success is not dependent upon your environment, but it is dependent upon how you view yourself!

If you think you are a failure, *then you are!* If you think no one loves you or cares about you, then that's the way life will treat you. A negative, unrenewed mind, thought life, and attitude will cause you to live a negative, carnal lifestyle, because the *inward image* you think about yourself will be projected to the outside.

You must see yourself correctly, and the only way to do that is to view yourself through the eyes of God. You must see yourself from the perspective of the New Covenant, as a new creation, and stop identifying with the old man, the old you, the old nature, and the old habits.

My little children, for whom I labor in birth again until Christ is formed in you.

Galatians 4:19

God's will for every believer is that Christ and the image of Christ would be completely formed in us, that we be a *mirror image* of Christ, Who is the original overcomer. The reality of the *overcomer's image* in our lives develops as we daily read, meditate, and feed upon the Word of God.

Allow no one except God to program your life, categorize your value, or rate your potential.

It's time you began to walk in the freedom and the lifestyle produced by the reality of Christ in you, the Greater One dwelling in you.

And he said to them, Be careful what you are hearing. The measure [of thought and study] you give [to the truth you hear] will be the measure [of virtue and knowledge] that comes back to you, and more [besides] will be given to you who hear.

Mark 4:24 (AMP)

The entrance and unfolding of Your words gives light; it gives understanding — discernment and comprehension — to the simple.

Psalm 119:130 (AMP)

"Light" means wisdom, or understanding the Word. Without wisdom, or seeing how the Word can be applied in your everyday life, knowledge of the Word is unfruitful. Wisdom is understanding the promises of God so they become practical solutions to daily problems.

How can you effectively *apply* God's Word and kingdom principles in your life, unless you *understand* the Word? That is why daily meditation in God's Word is a basic essential for every Christian. Abraham Lincoln said, "If I had eight hours to chop down a tree, I would spend six hours sharpening the ax."

If the ax is blunt and you do not sharpen the blade — then greater strength and more effort must be applied to get the job done — but the reward given by wisdom and understanding is winning success.

Ecclesiastes 10:10 (Original Hebrew)

This Book of the Law shall not depart from your mouth, but you shall meditate in it day and night, that you may observe to do according to all that is written in it. For then you will make your way prosperous, and then you will have good success.

Joshua 1:8

These three keys will transform your worldly self-image to a godly one and your carnal lifestyle to one of holiness:

1. *Knowledge.* Find out who you really are in Christ and speak God's Word.

2. *Meditation.* Occupy your mind with the thoughts of God and think God's Word.

3. *Wisdom.* Put knowledge of God's Word into practice in your daily living. Act on God's Word in faith.

Paul saw things correctly:

. . . Christ in you, the hope of glory.

Colossians 1:27

I have fought the good fight, I have finished the race, I have kept the faith.

Second Timothy 4:7

Paul had an *overcoming attitude!*

God is good!

God is big!

God is in control!

The key to developing a successful overcomer's image is to mediate on God's Word, especially verses relative to victory, success, and being Christ-inside minded.

Here are some aspects of scriptural meditation:

• to think on, consider, and ponder

• to envision yourself or imagine yourself with something not yet manifested

• to fix and focus your attention upon

• to mutter or to talk under your breath

• to chew over and over and digest

- to revolve in your mind

- to occupy your mind with God's opinion of you.

Meditation is a *thinking exercise.*

Take the Bible and begin developing a scriptural success image of yourself, the image of an overcomer in this life, bringing forth an overcomer's lifestyle. It is God's desire for you to be an overcomer, for you to succeed, and He has provided His Word and His Spirit to do so.

It is up to *you* to begin developing a greater image of who you are in Christ Jesus and put yourself in the way of success!

Chapter Ten Review

1. Our success only comes through Christ.

2. Until you really believe you *can,* you *can't.*

3. What you have as an *inward image* will determine the direction, prosperity, and success of your life on the *outside.*

4. Do not concern yourself with the outward circumstances. Instead, work on changing your inward image.

5. A negative unrenewed mind, thought life, and attitude will cause you to live a negative, carnal lifestyle.

6. God's will through the new creation is that you be a *mirror image* of Christ.

7. The reality of the *overcomer's image* in your life develops as you daily read, meditate, and feed upon the Word of God.

8. The key to developing a successful overcomer's image is meditation of God's Word, especially selected verses relative to victory, success, and being Christ-inside minded.

Let the Word of Christ

dwell in you richly.

Appendix I
Thirty-One Scriptures
For Monthly Meditation

Day 1

But seek first the kingdom of God and His righteousness, and all these things shall be added to you.

Matthew 6:33

Day 2

I have strength for all things in Christ Who empowers me — I am ready for anything and equal to anything through Him Who infuses inner strength into me, that is, I am self-sufficient in Christ's sufficiency.

Philippians 4:13 (AMP)

Day 3

Do not be deceived, God is not mocked; for whatever a man sows, that he will also reap.

Galatians 6:7

Day 4

'Call to Me and I will answer you, and show you great and mighty things, which you do not know.'

Jeremiah 33:3

Day 5

Wisdom is the principal thing; Therefore get wisdom. And in all your getting, get understanding.

Exalt her, and she will promote you; She will bring you honor, when you embrace her.

Proverbs 4:7,8

Day 6

Jesus said to him, "If you can believe, all things are possible to him who believes."

Mark 9:23

Day 7

Fear not, for I am with you; Be not dismayed, for I am your God. I will strengthen you, Yes, I will help you, I will uphold you with My righteous right hand.

Isaiah 41:10

Day 8

"Give, and it will be given to you: good measure, pressed down, shaken together, and running over will be put into your bosom. For with the same measure that you use, it will be measured back to you."

Luke 6:38

Day 9

"Assuredly, I say to you, whatever you bind on earth will be bound in heaven, and whatever you loose on earth will be loosed in heaven."

Matthew 18:18

Day 10

No evil shall befall you, Nor shall any plague come near your dwelling;

For He shall give His angels charge over you, To keep you in all your ways.

Psalm 91:10,11

Day 11

Beloved, I pray that you may prosper in all things and be in health, just as your soul prospers.

Third John 2

Day 12

So shall My word be that goes forth from My mouth; It shall not return to Me void, But it shall accomplish what I please, And it shall prosper in the thing for which I sent it.

Isaiah 55:11

Day 13

If any of you lacks wisdom, let him ask of God, who gives to all liberally and without reproach, and it will be given to him.

James 1:5

Day 14

Thus says the Lord, your Redeemer, The Holy One of Israel: "I am the Lord your God, Who teaches you to profit, Who leads you by the way you should go."

Isaiah 48:17

Day 15

For God has not given us a spirit of fear, but of power and of love and of a sound mind.

Second Timothy 1:7

Day 16

"You did not choose Me, but I chose you and appointed you that you should go and bear fruit, and that your fruit should remain, that whatever you ask the Father in My name He may give you."

John 15:16

Day 17

But you, beloved, building yourselves up on your most holy faith, praying in the Holy Spirit.

Jude 20

Day 18

Therefore do not cast away your confidence, which has great reward.

For you have need of endurance, so that after you have done the will of God, you may receive the promise.

Hebrews 10:35,36

Day 19

Roll your works upon the Lord — commit and trust them wholly to Him; [He will cause your thoughts to become agreeable to His will, and] so shall your plans be established and succeed.

Proverbs 16:3 (AMP)

Day 20

"No weapon formed against you shall prosper, And every tongue which rises against you in judgment You shall condemn. This is the heritage of the servants of the Lord, And their righteousness is from Me," Says the Lord.

Isaiah 54:17

Day 21

Finally, brethren, whatever things are true, whatever things are noble, whatever things are just, whatever things are pure, whatever things are lovely, whatever things are of good report, if there is any virtue and if there is anything praiseworthy — meditate on these things.

Philippians 4:8

Day 22

"Bring all the tithes into the storehouse, That there may be food in My house, and prove Me now in this," Says the Lord of hosts, "If I will not open for you the windows of heaven And pour out for you such blessing That there will not be room enough to receive it.

"And I will rebuke the devourer for your sakes, So that he will not destroy the fruit of your ground, Nor shall the vine fail to bear fruit for you in the field," Says the Lord of hosts.

Malachi 3:10,11

Day 23

If you really fulfill the royal law according to the Scripture, "You shall love your neighbor as yourself," you do well.

James 2:8

Day 24

He who covers his sins will not prosper, But whoever confesses and forsakes them will have mercy.

Proverbs 28:13

Day 25

He who deals with a slack hand becomes poor, But the hand of the diligent makes one rich.

Proverbs 10:4

Day 26

It is the Lord Who goes before you; He will [march] with you; He will not fail you or let you go, or forsake you; [let there be no cowardice or flinching, but] fear not, neither become broken [in spirit] (depressed, dismayed and unnerved with alarm).

Deuteronomy 31:8 (AMP)

Day 27

No temptation has overtake you except such as is common to man; but God is faithful, who will not allow you to be tempted beyond what you are able, but with the temptation will also make the way of escape, that you may be able to bear it.

First Corinthians 10:13

Day 28

And God is able to make all grace (every favor and earthly blessing) come to you in abundance, so that you may always and under all circumstances and whatever the need, be self-sufficient — possessing enough to require no aid or support and furnished in abundance for every good work and charitable donation.

Second Corinthians 9:8 (AMP)

Day 29

Therefore submit to God. Resist the devil and he will flee from you.

James 4:7

Day 30

Pride goes before destruction, And a haughty spirit before a fall.

Proverbs 16:18

Day 31

Any enterprise is built by wise planning, becomes strong through common sense, and profits wonderfully by keeping abreast of the facts.

Proverbs 24:3,4 (TLB)

Appendix II
Foundation For A Winning Life

How to be born again

How to receive the Holy Spirit

How to grow spiritually

Know who you are in Christ

How To Receive Salvation And Be Born Again

"For God so loved the world that He gave His only begotten Son, that whoever believes in Him should not perish but have everlasting life."

John 3:16

For I am not ashamed of the gospel of Christ, for it is the power of God to salvation for everyone who believes.

Romans 1:16

Jesus answered and said to him, "Most assuredly, I say to you, unless one is born again, he cannot see the kingdom of God."

John 3:3

- If you died this second, do you have absolute assurance that you would go to heaven?
- Do you know where you stand with God?
- Do you have the peace of God in your life?
- Do you know God's love and forgiveness in salvation?
- Have you accepted Jesus Christ as your personal Savior and Lord?
- Are you born again?

These are searching questions which will affect your life for the rest of eternity. Today, I encourage you to make sure of your salvation, make sure you are born again, and receive eternal life through the Lord Jesus Christ.

For the wages of sin is death, but the gift of God is eternal life in Christ Jesus our Lord.

Romans 6:23

Here are some key Bible facts about salvation:

1. Everybody needs salvation because all men are dead spiritually, separated from God, lost sinners on the road to hell and eternal damnation.

All we like sheep have gone astray; We have turned, every one, to his own way; And the Lord has laid on Him the iniquity of us all.

Isaiah 53:6

. . . for all have sinned and fall short of the glory of God.

Romans 3:23

Therefore, just as through one man sin entered the world, and death through sin, and thus death spread to all men, because all sinned.

Romans 5:12

But we are all like an unclean thing, And all our righteousnesses are like filthy rags; We all fade as a leaf, And our iniquities, like the wind, Have taken us away.

Isaiah 64:6

2. Jesus Christ (not Buddha, Mohammed, Krishna, or any other religious leader) is the only Savior.

Jesus said to him, "I am the way, the truth and the life. No one comes to the Father except through Me."

John 14:6

"Nor is there salvation in any other, for there is no other name under heaven given among men by which we must be saved."

Acts 4:12

For there is one God and one Mediator between God and men, the Man Christ Jesus.

First Timothy 2:5

And she will bring forth a Son, and you shall call His name Jesus, for He will save His people from their sins.

Matthew 1:21

3. The gospel of Christ is good news, and the good news is that God loves you so much, He sent His only Son, Jesus Christ, to die on the cross and pay the price for your salvation.

But God demonstrates His own love toward us, in that while we were still sinners, Christ died for us.

Romans 5:8

This is a faithful saying and worthy of all acceptance, that Christ Jesus came into the world to save sinners.

First Timothy 1:15

For when we were still without strength, in due time Christ died for the ungodly.

Romans 5:6

". . . for the Son of Man has come to seek and to save that which was lost."

Luke 19:10

4. Being "born again" means to be born into the family of God; you are born again *spiritually* by receiving eternal life.

Therefore, if anyone is in Christ, he is a new creation; old things have passed away; behold, all things have become new.

Second Corinthians 5:17

Jesus answered and said to him, "Most assuredly, I say to you, unless one is born again, he cannot see the kingdom of God."

John 3:3

I will give you a new heart and put a new spirit within you.

Ezekiel 36:26

And this is the testimony: that God has given us eternal life, and this life is in His Son.

He who has the Son has life; he who does not have the Son of God does not have life.

First John 5:11,12

Being born again is a spiritual rebirth. You are born of the Spirit of God, and God's eternal life and nature are imparted to your spirit. Salvation only comes through receiving Christ as Lord of your life. It does not come by joining or attending a church, reading your Bible every day, saying prayers, doing good deeds, being moral and religious, or water baptism.

5. How can you be born again?

Being born again is a free gift received by faith — you don't work for it, you don't earn it, and you can never deserve it. God offers salvation to us not through any religious or good works, but only through our personal faith in Jesus Christ, the One Who paid the price for our sin on the cross and was resurrected to give us a new life.

For by grace you have been saved through faith, and that not of yourselves; it is the gift of God.

Ephesians 2:8

In order to be saved, we must acknowledge our sins and repent, believing Jesus died for us and rose again. We must receive the risen Christ by faith as our personal Savior, and we must publicly confess Him as our Lord.

First, come to Jesus Christ in repentance, admitting your need of salvation.

"I tell you, no; but unless you repent you will all likewise perish."

Luke 13:3

And saying, "The time is fulfilled, and the kingdom of God is at hand. Repent, and believe in the gospel."

Mark 1:15

Repent therefore and be converted, that your sins may be blotted out.

Acts 3:19

Truly, these times of ignorance God overlooked, but now commands all men everywhere to repent.

Acts 17:30

To "repent" means you realize the wrong of sin and you make a 180-degree change in your thinking. True repentance involves a change in thinking, a change in direction which soon produces a complete change in lifestyle.

Second, believe in the gospel and the finished work of Jesus Christ on the cross.

For God so loved the world that He gave His only begotten Son, that whoever believes in Him should not perish but have everlasting life.

John 3:16

So they said, "Believe on the Lord Jesus Christ, and you will be saved."

Acts 16:31

"Most assuredly, I say to you, he who hears My word and believes in Him who sent Me has everlasting life, and shall not come into judgment, but has passed from death into life."

John 5:24

Third, through prayer, receive Jesus Christ personally into your life by faith.

But as many as received Him, to them He gave the right to become children of God, even to those who believe in His name.

John 1:12

For "whoever calls upon the name of the Lord shall be saved."

Romans 10:13

To make Jesus Christ your Lord, pray this prayer and believe right now:

"Father in heaven, I've heard Your Word and I want to be born again. Jesus, cleanse me of my sins and be my Lord and Savior. I want to be a child of God. I give my life to You right now. Thank you for making me a new person.

God, I believe I'm now born again because Your Word says I am. Jesus is my Lord. Thank You, Jesus, for a new life. Amen."

Now, don't go by what you think or feel. Go by what God's Word says. You are saved! Believe it!

Fourth, confess before God and men the Lordship of Jesus Christ.

Jesus was not ashamed or embarrassed to publicly die for you; therefore you should not be ashamed or embarrassed to publicly confess Jesus and share your testimony with people you know and those you meet in the future.

that if you confess with your mouth the Lord Jesus and believe in your heart that God has raised Him from the dead, you will be saved.

For with the heart one believes to righteousness, and with the mouth confession is made to salvation.

Romans 10:9,10

Once you have prayed and made your decision for Christ, write to me and I will send you more information to help you in following Jesus.

How To Receive
The Baptism In The Holy Spirit

"I indeed baptize you with water unto repentance, but He who is coming after me is mightier than I, whose sandals I am not worthy to carry. He will baptize you with the Holy Spirit and fire."

Matthew 3:11

The baptism in the Holy Spirit is a supernatural equipping with power from heaven, empowering the Christian for effective witness and service. It is evidenced by the believer speaking in a language given by the Holy Spirit and unknown to the one speaking.

"But you shall receive power when the Holy Spirit has come upon you; and you shall be witnesses to Me in Jerusalem, and in all Judaea and Samaria, and to the end of the earth."

Acts 1:8

And they were all filled with the Holy Spirit and began to speak with other tongues, as the Spirit gave them utterance.

Acts 2:4

The baptism in the Holy Spirit enables the Christian to build up his own spiritual life by direct communion with God, and it is the doorway to the nine supernatural gifts of the Spirit. In the New Testament Church, the experience of the baptism in the Holy Spirit was *normal* for all believers and was the next step after being born again.

"Behold, I send the Promise of My Father upon you; but tarry in the city of Jerusalem until you are endued with power from on high."

Luke 24:49

God's gift to the sinner is salvation and eternal life in Jesus Christ. His gift to the believer is the baptism in the Holy Spirit, with the evidence of speaking in tongues.

"I indeed baptize you with water, but He will baptize you with the Holy Spirit."

Mark 1: 8

"for John truly baptized with water, but you shall be baptized with the Holy Spirit not many days from now."

Acts 1:5

Here are some key Bible facts about the baptism in the Holy Spirit:

- The baptism in the Holy Spirit is a separate experience following salvation. (Acts 8:12-17).

- The baptism in the Holy Spirit is for every Christian, received by faith. (Luke 11:13; Acts 2:38,39).

- The Lord Jesus Christ is the Baptizer in the Holy Spirit. (Matthew 3:11).

- Jesus promised all believers rivers of living water — the Bible experience of being baptized in the Holy Spirit. (John 7:38).

- Receiving the baptism in the Holy Spirit is accompanied by the believer speaking in tongues. (Acts 10:44-46).

Jesus offered us a new way to live, but He also offered the power of the Holy Spirit to live His way of life. You don't beg for the Holy Spirit, or for the heavenly language. You simply ask for it and believe you receive it, based on what God's Word promises.

First, make sure you are born again and that you have a personal relationship with the Lord Jesus Christ.

Second, believe God's promises and be determined to act upon what the Scriptures say.

"If you then, being evil, know how to give good gifts to your children, how much more will your heavenly Father give the Holy Spirit to those who ask Him!"

Luke 11:13

Then Peter said to them, "Repent, and let every one of you be baptized in the name of Jesus Christ for the remission of sins; and you shall receive the gift of the Holy Spirit.

"For the promise is to you and to your children, and to all who are afar off, as many as the Lord our God will call."

Acts 2:38,39

Third, ask Jesus to baptize you with the Holy Spirit, believe that He does, and open your mouth and begin speaking in tongues as the Holy Spirit prompts you and gives the ability.

And they were all filled with the Holy Spirit and began to speak with other tongues, as the Spirit gave them utterance.

Acts 2:4

For they heard them speak with tongues and magnify God.

Acts 10:46

Pray this prayer right now and receive:

"Heavenly Father, I believe Your Word is true. I'm just going to believe Your words with childlike faith. Jesus, the Word says that You are the Baptizer, so I'm asking You to baptize me in the precious Holy Spirit. I believe I am receiving right now. The Holy Spirit is within me, and by faith, I release Him. Holy Spirit, rise within me as I praise my God. I expect to speak in tongues as You give me utterance."

Now begin to praise and worship God, vocalizing the sounds and utterances coming to your thoughts. Speak them out loud. Faith is an act! Just speak the syllables on your lips. You are speaking in a new tongue.

It sounds like gibberish? It's repetitive? Don't go by what it sounds like or what it feels like. Go by what the Bible says about it. It is a promise. It's yours. You have done what the *Bible* has told you to do.

Continue praying to God in tongues and expect to know and experience the Comforter, the Intercessor, the Counselor, the Advocate, the Strengthener, the Standby, and the Source of Power as you never have before!

Until you become accustomed to this new experience in the Lord, remember that Satan will come to try to steal this word from you (Matthew 13:4). He does not want you to grow in the power of the Holy Spirit, be a more effective witness, or move in the gifts of the Spirit!

Therefore, you can expect the devil to attack your mind with doubt and unbelief in an attempt to convince you that your experience isn't authentic. He will sometimes even use other believers to challenge the scriptural validity of the baptism of the Holy Spirit. Stand by what the Bible tells you about it!

Jesus said it as a simple command:

Go ye into all the world and preach the good news to all creation.

And these signs will accompany those who believe;

In my name they will drive out demons; they will speak in new languages.

Mark 16:15-17 NIV & AMP

What are the benefits and reasons for speaking in tongues?

1. Speaking in tongues causes your spirit man to be edified and built up.

He who speaks in a tongue edifies himself.

First Corinthians 14:4

But you, beloved, building yourselves up on your most holy faith, praying in the Holy Spirit.

Jude 20

2. Speaking in tongues is a supernatural means of giving God thanks, praise, and worship.

For they heard them speak with tongues and magnify God.

Acts 10:46

"God is Spirit, and those who worship Him must worship in spirit and truth."

John 4:24

3. Speaking in tongues enables you to pray and intercede for things and unknown situations when you don't know how to pray.

Likewise the Spirit also helps in our weaknesses. For we do not know what we should pray for as we ought, but the Spirit Himself makes intercession for us with groanings which cannot be uttered.

Romans 8:26

4. Speaking in tongues causes your spirit to be rested and refreshed.

For with stammering lips and another tongue He will speak to this people,

To whom He said, "This is the rest with which You may cause the weary to rest," And, "This is the refreshing."

Isaiah 28:11,12

5. Speaking in tongues causes the gifts, power, and anointing of God to be released in your life. (Read First Corinthians 12:1-11).

Child of God, take time every day to pray in tongues and enjoy these wonderful benefits!

How To Grow In The Christian Life

... but grow in the grace and knowledge of our Lord and Savior Jesus Christ. To Him be the glory both now and forever. Amen.

Second Peter 3:18

Now that you are born again and you have accepted the Lord Jesus Christ, it is essential that you grow spiritually. Applying the principles below and making them a part of your daily life will ensure your successful spiritual growth and bring peace, victory, fruitfulness, direction, and the blessings of God into your life.

1. Make sure you have made Jesus Christ Lord over every part of your life, that you have totally surrendered your life to Him.

"Only fear the Lord, and serve Him in truth with all your heart; for consider what great things He has done for you."

First Samuel 12:24

2. Renounce every association with groups who do not profess Jesus as Lord and the Bible as the Word of God.

... how you turned to God from idols to serve the living and true God.

First Thessalonians 1:9

And many who had believed came confessing and telling their deeds.

Also, many of those who had practiced magic brought their books together and burned them in the sight of all. And they counted up the value of them, and it totaled fifty thousand pieces of silver.

Acts 19:18,19

3. Receive the baptism in the Holy Spirit with the Bible evidence of speaking in tongues.

4. Obey Christ's command and be baptized in water, giving public testimony of your new life in Christ.

"Go therefore and make disciples of all the nations, baptizing them in the name of the Father and of the Son and of the Holy Spirit."

Matthew 28:19

Then Peter said to them, "Repent, and let every one of you be baptized in the name of Jesus Christ for the remission of sins; and you shall receive the gift of the Holy Spirit."

Acts 2:38

Making Jesus Christ Lord of your life produces an *inward* change in your heart. Being baptized in water is an *outward* act of obedience by which the believer testifies of the change that has taken place *inwardly.* By following Jesus in water baptism, we are *identifying* with His death, burial, and glorious resurrection, and we are making a public confession of our faith in Him.

Baptism in water is a natural symbol of the spiritual reality of salvation. Our life of sin and defeat is crucified and buried with Him as we are immersed in the water, and we emerge from the water in His resurrection, to lead a new life of righteousness and victory in Christ.

5. Read and study your Bible everyday (begin with fifteen minutes).

as newborn babes, desire the pure milk of the word, that you may grow thereby.

First Peter 2:2

Get yourself a *New King James Version,* a *New International Version,* or *The Living Bible.* Later, you may want to get *The*

Amplified Bible or a *New American Standard Bible.* There are Bibles available in church bookstores that contain a reading plan to help you systematically go through the Bible in one year.

> Your word is a lamp to my feet And a light to my path.
>
> Psalm 119:105

> So then faith comes by hearing, and hearing by the word of God.
>
> Romans 10:17

> But He answered and said, "It is written, Man shall not live by bread alone, but by every word that proceeds from the mouth of God."
>
> Matthew 4:4

Here are some pointers on how to read your Bible that can give you a good start.

- Establish a set time and place everyday to read.

- Ask the Holy Spirit to lead you, guide you, and teach you through God's Word.

- Follow a systematic plan of reading, don't just pick a page at random. Here is a suggested reading plan you can begin with, book by book: John, Acts, Romans, Mark, Galatians, Ephesians, Philippians, Colossians, and James. Also, read one Proverb and one Psalm a day. This plan will give you both wisdom and encouragement.

- Underline and mark meaningful verses that speak to you, especially God's promises. Color these verses and write in a notebook the things about which God speaks to you. Reading your Bible consistently will renew your mind, feed your spirit, and build your faith.

- Get into a Bible study group in your local church.

6. Spend time in prayer every day, talking to your heavenly Father.

"And in that day you will ask Me nothing. Most assuredly, I say to you, whatever you ask the Father in My name He will give you.

"Until now you have asked nothing in My name. Ask, and you will receive, that your joy may be full."

John 16:23,24

"Ask, and it will be given to you; seek, and you will find; knock, and it will be opened to you.

"For everyone who asks receives, and he who seeks finds, and to him who knocks it will be opened."

Matthew 7:7,8

The effective fervent prayer of a righteous man avails much.

James 5:16

New Testament prayer involves:

- Praising God for Who He is.
- Thanking God for what He has done in your life.
- Praying for your own needs and for other people (make a list).
- Praying in tongues to edify your spirit man.
- Listening to God. As you wait silently in His presence, He will speak to you.

7. Get rid and stay free of all unforgiveness, resentment, or bitterness toward anyone.

"And whenever you stand praying, if you have anything against anyone, forgive him, that your Father in heaven may also forgive you your trespasses.

"But if you do not forgive, neither will your Father in heaven forgive your trespasses."

Mark 11:25,26

To be forgiven we must forgive.

Unforgiveness opens the door to self-pity, hatred, anger, resentment, bitterness, depression, and many other problems which have a damaging effect on our lives spiritually, mentally, and physically.

Forgiveness is not an *emotion,* it is a *decision.* God never said we had to *feel* like forgiving, He has *commanded* us to forgive. Simply choose to forgive, release all bitterness, and by faith walk in love.

8. Join a New Testament church and fellowship with Christians regularly.

not forsaking the assembling of ourselves together, as is the manner of some, but exhorting one another, and so much the more as you see the Day approaching.

Hebrews 10:25

I was glad when they said to me, "Let us go into the house of the Lord."

Psalm 122:1

Find a strong local church that exalts Jesus Christ, preaches the Word of God uncompromisingly, and moves in the gifts of the Spirit. Attend church services every week, worshipping the Lord, and taking notes from the pastor's messages. It is important to submit to your pastor and church leadership, developing good friendships with God's people in the local church.

And they continued steadfastly in the apostles' doctrine and fellowship, in the breaking of bread, and in prayers.

Acts 2:42

9. Terminate wrong friendships and ungodly associations which hinder you, and form right relationships in the Body of Christ.

Do not be deceived: "Evil company corrupts good habits."
First Corinthians 15:33

He who walks with wise men will be wise, But the companion of fools will be destroyed.
Proverbs 13:20

Do not be unequally yoked together with unbelievers. For what fellowship has righteousness with lawlessness? And what communion has light with darkness?
Second Corinthians 6:14

Do you not know that friendship with the world is enmity with God? Whoever therefore wants to be a friend of the world makes himself an enemy of God.
James 4:4

Now that you are a Christian and a child of God, you cannot afford to spend time with old friends who seek to draw you back into a life of sin. Cut out any friendship, relationship, or association which hinders your spiritual life and progress in the kingdom of God. Do it today!

10. Put on the whole armor of God and resist temptation with the Word of God and the blood of Jesus.

No temptation has overtaken you except such as is common to man; but God is faithful, who will not allow you to be tempted beyond what you are able, but with the temptation will also make the way of escape, that you may be able to bear it.
First Corinthians 10:13

Therefore submit to God. Resist the devil and he will flee from you.

James 4:7

Read Ephesians 6:10-18.

Temptation is not a sin — yielding to the temptation is sin. Temptation always begins in our thoughts, so the key to victory is to resist it right there. We must discipline our thought lives with God's Word and refuse to give in to entertaining sinful thoughts.

But thanks be to God, Who gives us the victory — making us conquerors — through our Lord Jesus Christ.

First Corinthians 15:57 (AMP)

To successfully overcome temptation, we must guard ourselves from and avoid harmful, ungodly influences.

- Stay off the devil's territory — don't go to the places where he controls.

- Keep your spiritual life strong through the Word and prayer.

- Defeat every sinful thought with God's Word.

- Protect yourself from everything that would adversely affect you. Be selective with music, television, movies, books, and magazines.

11. Honor the Lord with your finances by giving the tithe (ten percent of your income) into your local church, and by giving offerings to ministries that preach and teach the Word of God uncompromisingly.

"Bring all the tithes into the storehouse, That there may be food in My house, And prove Me now in this," Says the Lord of hosts, "If I will not open for you the windows of heaven,

And pour out for you such blessing That there will not be room enough to receive it."

Malachi 3:10

Honor the Lord with your possessions, And with the first fruits of all your increase;

So your barns will be filled with plenty, And your vats will overflow with new wine.

Proverbs 3:9,10

"Give, and it will be given to you: good measure, pressed down, shaken together, and running over will be put into your bosom. For with the same measure that you use, it will be measured back to you."

Luke 6:38

Those who are taught the Word of God should help their teachers by paying them.

Galatians 6:6 (TLB)

Whatever ministry has sown spiritually into your life, has helped you, taught you, and fed you, it is your God-given responsibility to sow finances back into their ministry and support them.

12. Share your testimony, be a bold witness for Christ, and win souls.

"But you shall receive power when the Holy Spirit has come upon you; and you shall be witnesses to Me in Jerusalem, and in all Judaea and Samaria and to the end of the earth."

Acts 1:8

The fruit of the righteous is a tree of life, And he who wins souls is wise.

Proverbs 11:30

A true witness delivers souls.

Proverbs 14:25

let him know that he who turns a sinner from the error of his way will save a soul from death and cover a multitude of sins.

James 5:20

God's plan is that every born-again believer be filled with the Holy Spirit and then draw upon the power of God to witness to others about Jesus Christ. They should reach the unreached and tell the untold the good news message of the gospel.

Everyone of us should remember the eternal value of human souls and be faithful in witnessing. Christians who are faithful in witnessing will receive a reward from Christ Himself (First Peter 5:4). Because you are a witness in this life, you will have the joy of seeing the people who were won through your testimony when you get to heaven.

And He said to them, "Follow Me, and I will make you fishers of men."

Matthew 4:19

Growing in the Christian life checklist:

- Surrender every area of your life to Jesus Christ.
- Renounce every association with groups who do not profess Jesus as Lord and the Bible as the Word of God.
- Receive the baptism in the Holy Spirit.
- Be baptized in water as a public confession of Christ's Lordship in your life.
- Read and study the Bible every day.
- Spend time in prayer.

- Get rid of any unforgiveness and walk in forgiveness and love.
- Join a New Testament church.
- Terminate wrong friendships and ungodly associations.
- Put on the whole armor of God and resist temptation.
- Honor the Lord by giving your finances.
- Be a bold witness for Christ — share your testimony.

Knowing Who You Are In Christ

Now that you are a born-again Christian, God's Word tells you exactly *who you are in Christ* and *your rights* and *privileges* as a child of God.

I urge you right now to get your Bible, pen, notebook, and some colored pencils, and begin reading today from Romans, chapter 1, each day until you complete the epistles (the last one is Jude) of the New Testament. The epistles are God's love letters to His children, and as you read them, you will see the key phrases "in Christ," "in Him," "in whom," etc.

Take your colored pencils and mark these important verses in your Bible. They appear 150 times! In these scriptures, God is telling you w*ho you are* as a born-again believer in Christ.

Begin to *see, think,* and *talk* about yourself the way God does! By doing this, you will grow spiritually, your faith will develop, your self-image will greatly improve, and you will begin to experience victorious Christian living.

To help get you started, I have prepared a list of who you are in Christ from my own study of God's Word. *Mark* them in your Bible and *say* what God says about you.

Every born-again believer

- has been made *righteous* in Christ
  Second Corinthians 5:21

- has been *saved* by the blood of Jesus
  First Peter 1:18,19

- has been *delivered* out of Satan's kingdom
  Colossians 1:13

- has been *forgiven* and *set free* from condemnation
  Ephesians 1:7

- has been *cleansed* by the blood of Jesus
  First John 1:7

- has been *seated* with Christ in heavenly places
  Ephesians 2:6

- has been *blessed* with all spiritual blessings in Christ
  Ephesians 1:3

- has been *accepted* in the family of God through Christ
  Ephesians 1:6

- has been *reconciled* to God through Christ
  Second Corinthians 5:18

- has been *redeemed* from the slave market of sin
  Colossians 1:14

- has been *released* from the curse of the law
  Galatians 3:13

- has *inherited* the blessings of Abraham
  Galatians 3:29

- has been made a *king* and a *priest*
  Revelation 1:5,6

- has *eternal life*, the nature of God
  First John 5:13

- has *passed out of death into life*
  John 5:24

- has the *anointing* of God within him
  First John 2:27

- has been *predestined* to be conformed to image of Jesus
  Romans 8:29

- has been *called* with a holy calling
  Second Timothy 1:9

- is a *son* of God
  John 1:12

- has *overcoming power* through the blood of Jesus
  Revelation 12:11

- is a *member* of the royal priesthood
  First Peter 2:9

- is the *salt* of the earth
  Matthew 5:13

- is the *light* of the world
  Matthew 5:14

- is a *citizen* of heaven
  Philippians 3:20

- is an *ambassador* for Christ
  Second Corinthians 5:20

- is the *temple* of God
  First Corinthians 3:16

- is *saved by grace*
  Ephesians 2:8,9

- is a *child of light*
  Ephesians 5:8

- is *God's workmanship*
  Ephesians 2:10

- is *sanctified*
  First Corinthians 1:2

- is *inseparable* from God's Love
  Romans 8:38,39

Let Me Hear From You

I pray and believe that you have been encouraged and strengthened by the message of this book and it has caused you to grow spiritually. It always means a great deal to me to hear good reports and testimonies about how our teaching ministry is changing people's lives. So if you have been blessed and helped through this ministry, **please take time today to write me and share your words of encouragement.**

Also, when you write please pray about supporting our ministry financially so we can touch many more lives with the anointed message of God's Word.

If you feel that God is leading you to be involved in supporting this ministry, please fill out the following and along with your offering mail it to our address.

☐ Yes! I want to support your ministry with my monthly gift of $_____.

☐ Enclosed is my one-time gift of $_____.

☐ I am enclosing a special missions offering for the overseas outreaches of Norman Robertson Ministries $_____.

Thank you for your financial support, and I know that the seeds you have sown into this ministry will come back to you many times over. **(Luke 6:38)**

Name _____
(please print)
Address _____
City _____
State _____ Zip _____
Phone _____

Tear out this page and mail it to:
Norman Robertson Ministries
P. O. Box 3330
Matthews, North Carolina 28106

Prayer Changes Things

The challenges people face today are genuine and can be very difficult — fears, marriage and family problems, financial needs, depression, struggling with sickness, a lack of wisdom, difficulties in personal relationships and much more. Because we care about people and know the power of God released through faith and prayer can change your circumstances, it is the desire of my wife, Eleanor, and me to stand with you in prayer.

Perhaps you are facing difficult situations, discouragement and pressures in your life right now. **I encourage you to take action by writing to us and sharing your needs with us.** Together, we will release our faith and believe that God will intervene on your behalf!

> *Let us therefore come boldly to the throne of grace, that we may obtain mercy and find grace to help in time of need.*
>
> **Hebrews 4:16**

Regardless of your situation, take a moment to write and share your special needs with us. When you send in your prayer requests, sow your seed-faith offering towards your desired harvest.

Norman Robertson Ministries
P. O. Box 3330
Matthews, North Carolina 28106